CW00687818

# the prisoner

## AN ILLUSTRATED HISTORY

Original edition first published 2007 by Network Distributing Ltd. Reprinted 2008.
This new, illustrated edition first published 2017 by Network Distributing Ltd.
Text © 2017, Andrew Pixley.

ISBN 978-0-9929766-2-0

# the Prisoner

## AN ILLUSTRATED HISTORY

written by ANDREW PIXLEY

network

"They have written many feeble books on *The Prisoner*, and they have analysed that which never should have been," said Patrick McGoohan – the show's star, executive producer, often writer and director and creative force – to *Entrevue* magazine in January 1997. The show's co-creator and script editor George Markstein was also scathing about the over-analysis of the series which had started prior to his death in 1987. Over the fifty years since it first appeared, many different analyses have been published, offering conflicting points of view. Much of it can never be explained, but McGoohan's stated aim *was* to ignite thought in the viewer …

The following text is a revised abridgement of a set of viewing notes originally published in 2007 for the fortieth anniversary of the show's debut. It does not set out to analyse meaning in *The Prisoner* beyond comments made by those involved with its production and development. It is not prescriptive as to what the show is about, but a commentary of how it was made and originally received, with a focus on the period from 1965 to 1976, after which television seemed to become worthy of discussion and study. Since 1977, the appreciation society Six of One has published much analysis concerning the series, and from 2002 The Unmutual website has also been active in promoting the show. Various groups have also staged events where *The Prisoner* has been celebrated and dissected. Now popular culture has attained respectable status, academic works also delve into the phenomena.

It is a series which never fails to captivate me with its style and imagination whenever I revisit it, and the words which I wrote in 2007 still hold true: if you have never seen *The Prisoner*, you are in for a treat.

Be seeing you.

**Andrew Pixley, 2017**

# 1: "AFTER JOHN DRAKE – WHAT?"

*'After John Drake – what? This was the question asked on all sides when Patrick McGoohan came to an end of the* Danger Man *series – a series acclaimed in almost every corner of the world and one which turned McGoohan into one of the greatest names in television.'* – ITC Publicity, 1967

The story of *The Prisoner* effectively revolves around one man. Born in Astoria in Queens, New York at 4.31am on 19 March 1928, Patrick Joseph McGoohan left the USA when he was a few months old as his immigrant family returned to their farm in County Leitrim in Ireland, before moving to Sheffield in England. After studying at Leicester's Ratcliffe College, McGoohan worked with the British Rope Company in Sheffield and dabbled in amateur dramatics, making an early stage appearance in St Vincent's Youth Club's production of *Pride and Prejudice* at Easter 1945. He joined the Sheffield Playhouse repertory company in 1948, having had a variety of day jobs including working as a clerk at the National Provincial Bank. By 22, he was a star at the Playhouse where he met Joan Drummond, whom he married on Saturday 19 May 1951.

McGoohan's career continued with companies including the Bristol Old Vic, and by 1952 he had small roles in the West End, dabbling with directing on *Grace and Favour*, staged at the Q Theatre in July 1954. Monday

19 April 1954 saw his first television appearance – a live edition of the BBC historical dramatisation series *You Are There*. Soon he was working on films like *Passage Home*, while also getting a West End lead in *Serious Charge* at the Garrick in February 1955. The Rank Organisation spotted his talent, engaging him on films for five years in 1956, a contract prematurely truncated when financial problems hit the company and McGoohan became unhappy. On Tuesday 30 December 1958, McGoohan starred as Charles Castle in *The Big Knife* in Associated-Rediffusion's *Play of the Week* – a networked broadcast which brought him to the attention of Lew Grade.

Cigar-smoking entertainment mogul Lew Grade had launched his first theatrical agency in 1937. By 1954, Grade was in at the birth of commercial television in the UK, assembling the Incorporated Television Programme Company (ITP) which formed close links with Associated TeleVision (ATV), the franchise operating in London at weekends from September 1955 and the Midlands on weekdays from March 1956. A major part of ATV's success was the financing and distribution of filmed adventure series such as *The Adventures of Robin Hood*. In July 1957, US distributor Jack Wrather formed the Independent Television Corp in association with both ATV and ITP. In October 1958, ATV bought out ITP, then in February 1960 would buy out Wrather to totally own ITC, now a major distributor of British and American film series.

Following an acclaimed performance as Henrik Ibsen's *Brand* at the Lyric from April 1959, McGoohan was signed by ATV to star as freelance/ NATO security operative John Drake in *Danger Man*, a 35mm television film series. Following location shooting in North Wales from Monday 28 September, production on the 39 half-hour shows began at MGM British Studios in Borehamwood, north of London, on Monday 12 October. From the outset, McGoohan insisted on making Drake into what he felt was an acceptable family television hero. "When I was first asked to play John Drake, he was a fast-talking, amoral, slick guy, a violent gun-slinging, sexy type. You know – a woman in every bedroom," he told Warwick Charlton in *TV World* (17-23 October 1964). Aspects of overt violence and womanising were excised by McGoohan. "I abhor violence and cheap sex," he told Jeannie Sakol in *Cosmopolitan* in December 1969. "It is my view that a hero be a good man." By the early 1960s, McGoohan had three daughters – and strong feelings on what they should see on television.

On *Danger Man*, McGoohan struck up a friendship with assistant director David Tomblin. The pair established a production company, Keystone Films, in August 1960, later renaming it Everyman Films – a term meaning an individual with whom an audience can identify, coined by the sixteenth century English morality play *Everyman*. Born in Borehamwood in 1931, Tomblin

David Tomblin, pictured on the set of *Living in Harmony*

had worked in the film industry since he was 14. "David Tomblin and I became great friends instantly on the first location of *Danger Man*," commented McGoohan in an interview recorded with his daughter, Catherine, for the documentary *Six into One: The Prisoner File* in December 1983: "David and I used to knock ideas around for all sorts of things, round a *Prisoner*-type theme, so I suppose he was my closest associate."

Before production completed in early August, McGoohan directed the episode *Vacation* in July 1960. *Danger Man* debuted on ATV London and other areas on Sunday 11 September. In January 1961, Grade sold it to the American CBS network for screening from Wednesday 5 April 1961. In Autumn 1961, McGoohan refused the role of James Bond in the film *Dr No*, telling John Farrell of the Catholic magazine *Annunciation* (January 1966), "I didn't want it. Analyse the character. Take away the super-armament, the muscle, the glamour, the sex – what's left? Nothing."

Television drama moved towards the hour-long format. ITC's first such venture was *Ghost Squad*, a co-production with Rank, shooting at Beaconsfield from August 1961. In early 1962, Grade favoured McGoohan as Simon Templar in ITC's adaptation of *The Saint*. However, on Wednesday 2 May the *Daily Express* announced that McGoohan had rejected the part, commenting: "They have made *The Saint* just another private eye. I visualise him as a gay, romantic swashbuckler." Later, he told Dave Hanington of *TV Radio Mirror* (August 1966): "I refused because I thought – and still think – that the character's a rogue. A rat. And a wicked influence on anyone who tries to live decently."

From 1962, McGoohan made a couple of UK-based Walt Disney films. He went to Hollywood briefly, but disliked the scripts offered to him

Behind the camera on
*Danger Man*

and after five days missed his family. "I am not impressed by the trappings of stardom," he told *TV World* (17-23 October 1964).

Following the success of Roger Moore as *The Saint*, in mid-November 1963 Grade announced that *Danger Man* would re-enter production at MGM the following spring, this time as 26 one-hour episodes. Shooting began on Monday 9 March 1964, and Drake now operated out of the London offices of M9. Between June and October, Tomblin returned to the series as assistant director. The episode *Colony Three* by Donald Jonson, filmed in July, was retrospectively interesting. The Cold War narrative saw Drake taken to a remote, escape-proof English-style 'New Town' development in a communist country where foreign agents were trained to infiltrate into British society and all conversations were monitored. "Once people have entered Colony Three, they cease to exist," Drake was told.

Regions like ATV London debuted the reformatted *Danger Man* at 7.25pm on Saturday nights from 10 October; ATV Midlands relayed the same episode at 8pm the following Tuesday. Having filmed eighteen episodes, the crew took a week's break before resuming on Monday 14 December, knowing that the show was performing well on ITV.

On Monday 1 March 1965, ATV announced that McGoohan was now the highest paid TV star in Britain; CBS had paid £416,000 for 24 episodes of *Danger Man* which they would be retitling *Secret Agent*. This debuted on Saturday 3 April 1965, packaged with a theme song including the lyric: "They've given you a number/And taken 'way your name."

On Tuesday 2 March, production halted when MGM carpenters staged a walk out. Following the completion of the twenty-sixth episode on Friday 9 April, *Danger Man* relocated to Shepperton Studios. McGoohan flew

US title card for *Secret Agent*.

The *Danger Man* episode, *Colony Three*, anticipating themes in *The Prisoner*

Setting up a shot on *Danger Man* and, opposite, George Markstein.
Below: Series publicity brochure

to New York to make personal appearances the next day, and *Secret Agent* performed strongly on CBS. Meanwhile, *Danger Man* took a break on ITV after Saturday 13 March.

Six further shows were filmed at Shepperton from Monday 26 April to Friday 16 July. At the start of June, a delighted CBS ordered 26 more, as Grade announced that in future *all* of ATV's film series were to be shot in colour; prior to this, a few items such as *The Adventures of Sir Lancelot* had been made in this manner since late 1956. NBC had announced that its Fall 1965 schedule would be almost entirely in colour, forcing CBS and ABC to follow suit. Meanwhile UK broadcasters were still debating which colour technical standard to adopt.

Filming resumed on Monday 16 August when McGoohan directed *To Our Best Friend*; David Tomblin took over as second unit director from November. On CBS, *Secret Agent* aired through to Saturday 11 September 1965, while *Danger Man* resumed on ATV London at 7.25pm on Sunday 26 September, with ATV Midlands opting for 8pm on Thursdays.

The first inkling of McGoohan's next project appeared during publicity for *Danger Man*'s autumn return. Talking to Ian Sproat in the London listings magazine *TV Times* (9-15 October 1965), McGoohan voiced his concerns about the loss of individual identity: "You know, I fear by AD 2000 we'll all have numbers, no names." The actor was now in demand for other ventures. In a syndicated interview with Vince Leonard which appeared in papers such as the *Pittsburgh Press* (3 December 1965), he commented that he had "four feature productions in hand and another TV series. I won't be in it but produce it, instead." Ann Leslie's interview for the *Daily Express* (18 December 1965) noted that 'after the next series of *Danger Man* [McGoohan] will direct a series of 19 television scripts.'

CBS announced that *Secret Agent* would return as a mid-season replacement for the legal series *Trials of O'Brien* from Saturday 4 December, but in a syndicated interview with Joan Crosby which appeared in publications such as *The Bakersfield Californian* (25 December 1965), McGoohan commented of the series' future: "The network must let us know by March 11 if it wants additional episodes. If so, we will continue to film, but in color. But, if not, we won't do another season in England."

By 1966, *Danger Man* was a key ingredient of ITC's healthy US sales. Three other shows had also been successfully marketed. The World War II US justice drama *Court Martial*, which had been made by Roncom at Pinewood through to August 1965 was being shown on ABC, as was *The Baron*, which had been shooting in colour at ABPC Elstree since July 1965. Finally, a colour pilot for *The Saint*, shot in November 1965, had resulted in a sale to

NBC, and production was to resume at ABPC in February 1966.

McGoohan then directed the *Danger Man* episode *The Paper Chase*, during which he was voted ITV Personality of the year by the Variety Club of Great Britain on Wednesday 9 February, with the awards ceremony televised on BBC1 on Tuesday 8 March.

He now considered projects over which he would have control, indicating to William Kritz in the *New York Times* (23 January 1966) that he was planning on filming *Brand*. Another venture was a pilot script for *Vagabond* (concerning adventurous drifter Johnny Quill) written by ATV script consultant Lewis Greifer. Born in London's East End in 1915, after serving with the RAF during the war, the left-wing Greifer became a journalist with the *Evening Standard* in 1952, moving into television and radio. From 1957 he wrote a number of serials for ATV, joined the company in 1962 and had been working on *Love Story*.

Wanting to write his own material, McGoohan needed an editor to help him, asking Greifer for advice. Greifer suggested his friend George Markstein, who joined *Danger Man* as script editor in early 1966, having worked on *Court Martial*. Born Gustav Georg Markstein in Berlin in August 1926, Markstein's family had come to Britain when he was a child. After working as a reporter for the *Southport Guardian* in the late 1940s, Markstein wrote for *The Overseas Weekly* and the US Air Force base newspaper *UK Eagle*. He contributed to the programme *Our American Cousins*, screened by Associated-Rediffusion on Tuesday 15 January 1957, and undertook further work for the broadcaster on the documentary series *This Week* and as script editor on the police drama *No Hiding Place* during 1961. From September to December 1965, Markstein had been a regular writer for the *TV Times*, usually on the themes of America (including *Court Martial*) and also broadcasting. Those who worked with Markstein recalled that he sometimes alluded to working with or for intelligence agencies; he was evasive about this, commenting to John Dunn on BBC Radio 2 (3 March 1986), "I've been in the same room as people like that [...] I did some work that required me to sign the Official Secrets' Act." "They both got on really well to start with," recalled Greifer of the McGoohan-Markstein partnership to Robert Fairclough in *The Prisoner: The Original Scripts – Volume 1* (Reynolds & Hearn, 2005).

McGoohan harboured ideas for his own series which would look at the freedom that an individual had within 1960s society. "The general theme of the man in isolation against authority and bureaucracy, the idea of being a rebel against suppression and stupid rules has been with me since I was able to start thinking about anything at all," he explained in 1983, "[the] idea was with me for many years before I put it together [...] and decided to do the series."

The issue of personal self-respect was of great concern to him. Speaking in *Cosmopolitan*, he explained that his new series was conceived as "an allegory … a fable … a protest against regimentation and loss of individuality."

"I've always been obsessed with the idea of prisons in a liberal democratic society," McGoohan told Joan Barthel in *TV Guide* (25-31 May 1968), "I believe in democracy, but the inherent danger is that with an excess of freedom in all directions we will eventually destroy ourselves." While many cited the influence of Franz Kafka on *The Prisoner*, McGoohan denied this, noting he only saw Orson Welles' 1962 film of Kafka's *The Trial* after he had made his series. The only influence McGoohan admitted to was George Orwell's landmark 1948 novel of a totalitarian future. "I wrote it with *1984* in mind," he told

Mike Bygrave in *You: The Mail on Sunday Magazine* (27 March 1983).

McGoohan's desire to convey thought-provoking statements was allied with an increasing ennui with *Danger Man*. "Boredom, was how it started," is what McGoohan told Warner Troyer when interviewed on TV Ontario in March 1977. Feeling Drake was becoming repetitious, the actor sought the challenge of his own Everyman Films project with himself as executive producer. "I worked very hard on *Danger Man* and gradually became more involved in the producing, writing and creative side of it," he told Mike Tomkies of *TV World* (25 November–1 December 1967). The actor was keen to branch out creatively, and direct more. "I also wanted to get some experience with cameras," McGoohan recalled of *Danger Man* to Tom Soter in *Video* (July 1985), "I used to spend every spare minute I'd got in the editing room."

The star voiced his desire to have more control to *Danger Man* producer Sidney Cole. Speaking to Al Samujh in Issue 49 of *The Danger Man Collection* (25 October 2006), Cole recounted, "Towards the end of *Danger Man* […] Pat said to me, 'Why does it always have to be the way you want it?' […] So I said, 'Well, it's very simple, Pat – I'm the producer.' And that inspired him to go off and see Lew Grade."

Although *Secret Agent* was nominated by the Hollywood Screen Producer's Guild as Best Produced Television Programme for 1965, by early March things were not going well for ITC in the USA. *The Baron* had debuted on ABC on Thursday 20 January, but by the end of February the US trade paper

*Variety* was reporting that the show was unlikely to continue for long. And now CBS had not followed up their stated intention to purchase colour episodes of *Danger Man*. After 45 hour-long adventures, production on *Danger Man* temporarily halted at MGM on Friday 4 March.

With *Danger Man*'s future uncertain, McGoohan discussed other ventures with Grade. According to director Pat Jackson, Grade suggested that the star should consider alternative proposals to bring to him over the coming days. In the intervening time, McGoohan found himself reluctantly taken along to a cocktail party by his wife, at which a Home Office official spoke to him about the problems of security surrounding former operatives. This was one of various tales arising about how McGoohan's next series would be inspired. Second assistant director Bernard Williams recalled a tale about a social function with security officials present to Chris Campbell in *Number Six* Issue 31 (Spring 1992), "When Patrick posed the question: 'What happens to agents who want to retire? What do you do with them?' they said, 'Well we have places to send them, to stop them from going across the border to other countries'." Camera operator Jack Lowin explained in the *Daily Sport* (7 September 1992), "[McGoohan] had read a book published in America about what happened to secret agents when they retired [which] told of a village in the States where these people were sent for security reasons."

This notion arose in conversations with George Markstein. One example of real-life security which Markstein discussed was Inverlair Lodge,

Above: Inverlair Lodge also provided the background for Markstein's 1974 novel, *The Cooler*

a remote venue nicknamed 'The Cooler' in Glen Spean, Inverness. "I had been doing some research into the Special Operations Executive (SOE) and I had come across a curious establishment that existed in Scotland during the War into which they put recalcitrant agents," explained Markstein to Chris Rodley for the Channel 4 documentary *Six into One: The Prisoner File* (16 January 1984). Built in 1730, the lodge had been requisitioned by the SOE in 1941 as their 'Number 6 Special Workshop School'. Markstein had talked with people who had been at Inverlair because they had been briefed with codes and information too valuable to allow them to defect or to be captured by the 'other side'. McGoohan seized on this notion that people could disappear in this manner with D notices to gag the media: he asked *TV Guide*, "What do you do with defectors, or with people who have top-secret knowledge of the highest order and who, for one reason or another, want out? Do you shoot them? I know there are places where these people are kept. Not voluntarily, and in absolute luxury. There are three in this country – let

someone deny it." Markstein and McGoohan initially conceived of their penitentiary as being on an island.

Speaking to *TV World* (25 November–1 December 1967), McGoohan posed similar questions: "Imagine you are a scientist who is working on a top-secret project, like the first rocket trip to Mars. And suddenly you decide: 'I'm going to resign. I want a holiday.' You have vital information in your head [...] information that could change the future course of the world [...] Tremendous pressures are put upon you – whether by the side who is trying to get your secrets or by the side who has lost you and must prevent that knowledge getting out. A man like this has to live under wraps. His individuality, and even his sanity, is constantly threatened."

A close shave? Drake and gadget in *You're Not In Any Trouble, Are You?*

*The Prisoner* itself is a confusing and often contradictory show; its background is no more straightforward, as recollections diverge. Markstein claimed that he thought up the series format while travelling home on the 6.21pm from Shepperton to Waterloo. Interviewed for *Six into One* he said, "One of the things I didn't know was what to call it, so I ended up calling it *The Prisoner*." With regards the series' title, McGoohan had previously appeared in a BBC TV presentation of Bridget Boland's religious and political play *The Prisoner*, playing the Interrogator; the play was recorded on Thursday 21 February 1963 and screened on Sunday 24 February as part of *The Sunday Night Play*.

Both McGoohan and Markstein claimed the mantle of creator of *The Prisoner*. Examining their comments, it is clear that both men's input was essential to the series. While the heart and soul stemmed from McGoohan's personal feelings, the initial structure and format built upon material put forward by Markstein.

Markstein's vision for *The Prisoner* concerned an SOE-type prison situated in a limbo. Interviewed for *Six into One*, he said that he "typed a couple of pages. They were about a secret agent – and after all Drake had been a secret agent – who suddenly quits without any apparent reason, as McGoohan had quit without any apparent reason, and who is put away!" The script editor saw the show as directly paralleling McGoohan's desire to resign from *Dan-*

*ger Man*. "I was very hooked on this Kafkaesque idea of the spy who cannot escape his fate," Markstein told John Dunn, "What I intended, originally, was that McGoohan is held by people and he doesn't know which side he's working for." In *Channel 13 Review* (May 1978), Markstein noted of the concept: "I've always been interested in the fact that all people are prisoners […] A movie star is the prisoner of his face […] What happens to a secret agent who is in possession of sensitive knowledge and wants to retire? Everyone thinks there's an ulterior motive – you're writing a hot memoir or selling out to the other side."

McGoohan's dehumanising element was manifested by those in the establishment being only referred to as numbers – the central character being Number 6. McGoohan told Barrington Calia in *New Video* Magazine (July 1985), "Six is the only number which becomes another number when inverted. Turn it upside down and it becomes 'nine'. I liked it for that reason." Speaking to Judith Regan in *The Press* (Christchurch: 30 December 1982), Markstein declared: "I decided to call him No. 6 because it's high enough to make him important and low enough for him to get pushed around." The unseen controller of the prison would be Number 1.

Number 6's identity was another minefield. "Of *course* he was Drake," Markstein told Roger Langley in Six of One's *Escape* Issue 3 (Summer 1982). Drake had been created by *Danger Man*'s original producer Ralph Smart, but McGoohan wanted the show to be his own creation. As Markstein explained to John Dunn, "I wanted to call the Prisoner 'John Drake' originally, because my idea was that John Drake had resigned, as Pat had resigned [from *Danger Man*]. McGoohan loved the idea. Then he screamed, 'My god! John Drake! That means we will have to pay Ralph Smart royalties'." McGoohan's *Danger Man* stunt double, Frank Maher heard about the project after an evening game of squash with McGoohan. "I asked him if it was supposed to be John Drake," he told Larry Hall and Arabella McIntyre-Brown in *Number Six* Issue 13 (Autumn 1987), "and he said it was, although this wasn't going to be stated." The series' film librarian Tony Sloman recalled of early episodes in the documentary *Don't Knock Yourself Out* (Network, 2007): "On the continuity sheets, instead of 'P' for 'Prisoner' it still said 'Drake'."

"John Drake did not become the Prisoner. I know a lot of people who thought so, and I don't blame them," McGoohan said in 1983, adding that Number 6 "was meant to represent anyone […] in a position where they had access to vital information of national importance [… Number 6] was not necessarily a secret agent. He was never *called* John Drake, he just happened to look like him." As for Number 6's reasons for resigning, McGoohan told *New Video*: "He simply resigns as a matter of choice. He shouldn't have to answer to anyone. It's entirely his prerogative, his God-given right as an individual to proceed in any way he sees fit. That's the whole point of it all." In the series, Number 6's behaviour, habits and dress sense echoed Drake ... and Mc-Goohan. "Of course McGoohan contributed greatly; he *was* Number 6," said Markstein in *Escape*.

McGoohan and Markstein quickly settled on a real-life location for their 'Village' where Number 6 would be ensnared: Portmeirion in Gwynedd, North Wales. "It came out of a [Sunday magazine article], because of the unbelievable styles of architecture. One wanted a place that was completely and utterly baffling," explained Markstein to John Dunn. Portmeirion was well known to McGoohan who told Roger Goodman in April 1979, "I went on holiday with my wife and children to Portmeirion and saw what I thought was a very unusual place." Around September 1959, Portmeirion had been used for filming on *Danger Man*, when its startling Mediterranean construction featured in episodes like *View from the Villa* and *Under the Lake*. "I was astounded and longed to find out more about it," McGoohan recalled in 1983, "I met Clough Williams-Ellis, the architect, and he talked at great length and showed me around and told me about his dream, this thing that he had designed."

Two of the original recce stills taken by Bernie Williams and Leslie Gilliat in June 1966

Portmeirion grew out of a small late eighteenth century industrial port called Aber Iâ ('Frozen Estuary') situated in a cove. The venue was developed in the nineteenth century with exotic plantings and a number of buildings (later becoming the main hotel, Mermaid cottage and Salutation restaurant) completed by 1862. Born in May 1883, Clough Williams-Ellis was a renowned architect who had dreamed of building his own village since he was a child. Looking for a suitable coastal site, he purchased the overgrown peninsula from his uncle for around £20,000 in 1925, renaming it Portmeirion (i.e. a port in the county Merionethshire). He erected buildings inspired by his travels in Italy and Austria, aiming to develop the land without defiling the natural contours of the beautiful countryside, creating a "light opera" of architecture. The exclusive hotel opened at Easter 1926, with more buildings added by 1939, and further construction from 1954. Clough salvaged distinctive architectural elements from around the country, rebuilding them in his hamlet. "The combination of this 'man in isolation' in the midst of this beautiful spot had a certain appeal for me," said McGoohan in 1983, "It could be made either into an island – with its long beach – or a village somewhere, anywhere, by virtue of its architecture, which was so mixed you wouldn't know where it was."

Unlike the ongoing series format of *Danger Man*, McGoohan envisaged *The Prisoner* as a self-contained narrative, telling Troyer he wanted to do "Seven [episodes], as a serial as opposed to a series. I thought the concept […] would sustain for only seven."

As producer, McGoohan naturally wanted David Tomblin – a business partner he could utterly rely on. Markstein quickly came to admire Tomblin's work, commenting in *Escape*, "David Tomblin was a very key man." With Tomblin and Markstein on board, McGoohan could now put his fears and feelings on film.

# 2: "IT'S SO CRAZY, IT MIGHT WORK"

Although CBS had not indicated interest in colour missions for John Drake, ITC investigated the possibility with colour test episodes as with *The Saint*. After a fortnight's break, Patrick McGoohan and the *Danger Man* team were back at Shepperton on Monday 21 March 1966 shooting *Koroshi*, a two-hour colour 'special' and potentially the start of a new series. In February 1966 a two-part narrative for *The Baron* (*Masquerade* and *The Killing*) began shooting at ABPC; this could air on television as two episodes, and as *The Man in a Looking Glass* – later be released theatrically – or as a TV movie. In 1965, ITC had attempted to syndicate TV movies assembled from episodes of the earlier series *Man of the World* and *The Sentimental Agent*.

*Danger Man*'s final monochrome edition aired on ATV London on Sunday 3 April and its conclusion was announced on Friday 15 April. "I am not fed up with *Danger Man*, but it has had a long run," McGoohan told Clifford Davis for his front page story (*Danger Man Quits After Four Years*) in the *Daily Mirror* (16 April 1966). In the bulletin, Lew Grade added: "Mr McGoohan and I are starting work on an entirely new TV film series in October. It is Mr McGoohan's own idea and will be a new kind of adventure programme." In the *Daily Mail*, Brian Dean reported that the two colour *Danger Man* episodes would air in the autumn, and that McGoohan had been 'signed up by ATV Network for a new thriller series to be made in colour this year'. In the *Daily Express*, Martin Jackson quoted the star describing his next venture as "another adventure series, but a very different sort of character. It promises to be very exciting." Grade added: "Mr. McGoohan is coming to see me tomorrow to discuss the details […] We have decided to take *Danger Man* off at the height of its popularity."

By now, Patrick McGoohan, George Markstein and David Tomblin had assembled a detailed pitch document covering all aspects of Village life for the meeting on Saturday 16 April. McGoohan felt that because he was in good-standing over *Danger Man*, he could sell *The Prisoner* to Grade as the impresario backed hunches. "He has an instinct. A feeling for something," explained McGoohan on BBC2's *The Persuader: The TV Times of Lord Lew Grade* (27 August 1994).

"I always saw Mr Grade on a Saturday morning between six and six-thirty," recalled McGoohan in 1983, "he used to get to the office at 6am and I have always been an early riser, so it was a good time for us to meet, and any business we had to discuss because […] you got a decision very quickly."

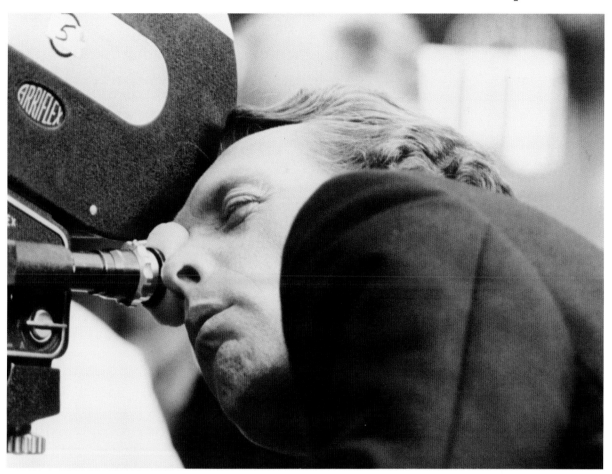

# Danger Man is ending four-year run

**By BRIAN DEAN**

THE ITV adventure series *Danger Man* is to be dropped after a four-year run.

*Daily Mail* (16 April 1966)

McGoohan on location with camera operator Len Harris

Grade was keen for McGoohan to make more ATV shows like *Danger Man*, offering a substantial deal. Instead the actor enthusiastically explained that he wanted to do something different, opening his briefcase of storylines, notes, photographs and budgets. "I pulled out this wad of paper. He looked somewhat horrified and said, 'You know I don't like to read all that. Can't you tell me about it?' So I talked to him for about fifteen minutes. He listened intently, as he always did, got up and walked up and down the office, puffing on his cigar, then said to me, 'You know, it's so crazy, it might work'."

Grade wanted to know when McGoohan could start. The star said that by retaining the *Danger Man* crew they could be ready to go quickly. "That was it – we shook hands. We never had a contract. It was a deal and from that moment on he gave me total freedom," recalled McGoohan. Grade backed his instincts with McGoohan, placing his trust in him. "He admits to this day that he doesn't know what [*The Prisoner*] was about," McGoohan told Howard Foy in *PrimeTime* Issue 16 (Winter 1990/1991). Speaking to Warner Troyer, McGoohan recalled Grade's promise: "The money'll be in your company's account on Monday morning."

McGoohan originally saw himself behind the camera on *The Prisoner* rather than in front. "I would've preferred someone else to play the role, but circumstances wouldn't have it that way," he told *New Video*, "I would much rather write and direct than act. As a director, I'm totally objective." Presumably, part of the deal with Grade was that the established international star would be the face to sell the venture.

Grade's backing and trust was a great burden of serious responsibility for McGoohan for the next two years. *The Prisoner* had a higher budget than its ITC stablemates; other shows could not afford the luxury of a month's filming away from London with principal actors, which the Everyman team were planning at Portmeirion. McGoohan wanted to put every penny he could on screen, telling *New Video*, "I took less pay than I was initially offered in exchange for a percentage of the profits."

Tomblin recalled McGoohan's news that Everyman had Grade's backing to Steven Ricks in *Number Six* Issue 30 (Winter 1992). "So I said, 'Oh great!' I wasn't quite sure what he was about, you know. So he said: 'Sit down and write the first episode'." This was Tomblin's first screenplay on which he worked with Markstein for a month. "They said 'leave us alone'," recalled McGoohan in 1983, "That was fine, because I was working on a script of my own." McGoohan's script, a potential second episode, was going to be a political satire on elections.

During the writing of the first script, *Arrival*, it was decided that the character of Number 2 – the figure implementing the orders of Number 1 – would regularly change rather than being a second recurring character as initially conceived. "I thought it would be a good idea [...] not so that you have a guest appearance of a good actor, but because the idea of the Village would be that you could never form a relationship," explained Tomblin in *Number Six*. Markstein likened this to changing of bank managers, where customers with a grievance would be confronted by a new figure, denying all knowledge of issues with their predecessor. "I think they disappeared without a trace," McGoohan told Troyer of the previous Number 2s.

McGoohan declared *Arrival* to be "the best pilot script I have ever read". He developed it further, explaining in 1983, "I asked them if they would mind if I put in a couple of things which they could throw out if they didn't like ... we just went a little further in certain areas – the political area for instance."

*The Prisoner* sealed the fate of *Danger Man*. "Before we finally finished [production], Pat came to my office and said he'd got a wonderful idea for a new series, and he wasn't going to do any more *Danger Man*," said Sidney Cole in *The Danger Man Collection*. Instead, Cole developed a format by Dennis Spooner and Richard Harris called *McGill* about an ex-intelligent agent turned bounty hunter. Meanwhile, McGoohan sounded out his colleagues about *The Prisoner*. In *Number Six*, Frank Maher recalled McGoohan telling him that both *The Prisoner* and *McGill* were starting: "He wanted to give me plenty of time to make up my mind which one to do. I made up my mind immediately to stay with him." McGoohan also employed Bernard Williams to help set up the new show.

Two Number Twos for the price of one ... Guy Doleman and George Baker in *Arrival*

Back at MGM, production on the colour episodes *Koroshi* and *Shinda Shima* continued, with McGoohan seeing these as a colour test for *The Prisoner*. On the morning of Tuesday 18 April, the BBC Home Service's *Today* programme carried a two minute report by Eveline Garratt who had interviewed McGoohan at Shepperton concerning Drake being 'retired'. Shooting wrapped on Friday 21 April, by which time ABC had announced a deal to buy *McGill* on the proviso that an American lead was cast.

Talking to Alix Palmer in the *Daily Express* on Wednesday 27 April, McGoohan commented "I know I have a debt to television which must be repaid." The actor's new series was described as 'Subject matter: secret' but it was noted that he was also working on a film and had plans for two plays – one in London and one on Broadway. In the *Kinematograph Weekly* trade paper (28 April 1966), columnist Tony Gruner reported: 'ATV [will] not be going ahead with further episodes of [*Danger Man*]. The company has in mind another film adventure show with McGoohan which they hoped to start with later this year.'

The final first-run *Secret Agent* appeared on CBS on Saturday 30 April, after which repeats were scheduled through to 10 September. On Tuesday 10 May, ATV announced that NBC would screen *The Saint* from January, and that the new McGoohan series ('the subject [is] still vague') would be made in the autumn. Grade then heralded further transatlantic ATV deals on Thursday 2 June, revealing the title of McGoohan's new series publicly as *The Prisoner* with a confirmation that it would be shot in colour, while *McGill* would film from August. Quoted in *Television Today* on Thursday 9 June, Grade said little about *The Prisoner* beyond: "It is a wholly new theme. I have never known anything as exciting as this ... it is absolutely brand new ... and a very expensive project." The announcement generated various articles around the world, such as *Pat McGoohan to Film New Action Program* in *The Pantagraph* in Bloomington, Illinois on Saturday 11 June.

Above: McGoohan with director Don Chaffey on location for *Arrival* and, opposite, working out the moves for *Checkmate*

For *The Prisoner*, McGoohan's team returned to MGM British in Borehamwood, close to the star's home in Mill Hill. The studios had been constructed as Amalgamated Studios in 1936 but never completed; it was then purchased by Metro-Goldwyn-Mayer in 1944, being made operational in April 1947. The largest of the Borehamwood studios at 120 acres, it had ten sound stages in all. Already shooting there were *2001: A Space Odyssey* and *The Dirty Dozen* (both scheduled to mid-October), while *Grand Prix* was to film interiors briefly in September.

Everyman approached director Don Chaffey to direct the first three months of episodes. "I used to like doing television in that way," explained Chaffey, interviewed for *Six into One*, "This would build up into a sort of rhythm and be the equivalent of a feature as far as I was concerned."

A man who prided himself on planning, Chaffey had frequently directed *Danger Man* since July 1964 and became friendly with McGoohan. Born in Hastings in 1917, Chaffey joined Gainsborough Films as a draughtsman and art director, made documentaries for GB Instructional and worked for the Children's Film Foundation. Moving into television films he directed episodes of *The Adventures of Robin Hood* and other ITC-distributed series, and then feature films including *Jason and the Argonauts*. "I first met Patrick McGoohan when Walt Disney asked me to direct *The Three Lives of Thomasina* [from August 1962]. I had seen him before [...] as a stage actor and knew his acting prowess," Don recalled for *Six into One*.

Chaffey was about to film *The Viking Queen* for Hammer Films at Ardmore Studios in Ireland from Monday 13 June 1966 when McGoohan approached him. "I said: 'Fine, you do what you like with it!' He said: 'No, I'd like you to direct the first episodes to set the style of it.' I just refused point blank and went off to Ireland," remembered Chaffey on *Six into One*. However, McGoohan gave the scripts to Chaffey's daughter, insisting that she had to get her father to look at them: "She said: 'You've got to read these, they're compulsive viewing. I reckon you're going to have eleven million people loving to hate you every Sunday night if you make them'." After *The Viking Queen* wrapped in mid-August, Chaffey would be free for *The Prisoner*.

Already there was conflict between script editor and executive producer. "[Markstein] thought, despite any amount of dissuasion, that it's got to be an extension [of *Danger Man*]," McGoohan told *PrimeTime*. He pointed out to Markstein the new show's hyper-real elements compared to its forebear's realism. In style, McGoohan wanted *The Prisoner* to be totally different to *Danger Man*. However, the series would still not feature sexual/romantic material nor the use of firearms; McGoohan wanted a family programme that children could watch.

The first three pages of *Arrival*'s shooting script covered the 'Standard Opening', a title sequence of nineteen images (scenes A to T) which set the series' background. The first shot was to be storm clouds from existing library material ('stock') with a 'jagged flare of lightning […] thunder merging into the high-pitched scream of a jet aircraft.' On 'a vast deserted runway', the 'jet scream fades to absolute silence' as a tiny spec hurtled towards the camera: 'It is a silver Lotus 7. It explodes into lens with the crack of the sound barrier being broken.' The next shot introduced the Prisoner, referred to throughout as 'P' (for Patrick/Prisoner). A high angle London panorama picked out 'the ant-like Lotus 7, darting angrily through traffic'. At an underground garage, 'a double-decker London Transport bus comes lumbering towards us. The Lotus emerges from behind it, overtakes and swerves across the front to disappear down into the bowels of an underground garage.' The next shot was in an 'Underground Lift Shaft' where 'the lift

drops like a stone'; P alighted, walking 'fast in determination down a long corridor', in and out of pools of light. He crashed through a door to see a man at a desk: 'formally dressed. Bureaucratic. The office is painted white.' P forcefully paced about, gesticulating: 'The language would be strong if we could hear what is being said. We can't. Instead each dynamic gesture is punctuated by a clap of thunder. The other man is still and thoughtful. He says nothing.' Before storming out, P threw an envelope from his pocket down on the desk. In a 'Computer Record Room […] a computer flicks rapidly through a stack of record cards. One card drops out onto a moving feeder belt. We see on it a photograph of P.' At an endless row of filing cabinets in a 'Filing Room', a drawer 'opens of its own volition.' The card was dropped in, the drawer snapped shut, bearing the label: 'Resigned.'

Following this, P drove up to his 'London Home' and entered, whereupon viewers would see 'the distant figure of a man giving a signal.' In his bedroom, P packed in a hurry, checking his watch; 'He appears to have a weight off his mind.' A holiday brochure and ticket could be seen. Outside, a hearse pulled up and 'Four men in proper attire get out and move purposefully to the front door.' Inside, P's suitcase was packed and his ticket was in his pocket when 'the door-bell peals. He moves to the window and looks out [to see] the standard London scene. Sun shines brightly.' Dropping the Venetian blind against the glare, P was turning to answer the door when, 'He is pole-axed in shock. His eyes go. He grabs at his throat. He staggers and falls on the divan beside the window.' A whip-pan showed a vapour jet hissing through the keyhole. This was followed by two helicopter shots; London was disappearing below and then the sea and a peninsula zooming up. P came to in his room. 'He rises and moves to the window for some air. He pulls the Venetian blind and looks out […] In place of the established London view we have a panorama of the village of Portmeirion.' As P looked in shock, the script indicated, 'Freeze Frame: Main Titles'. At the end of this sequence, it was noted, 'N.B. The standard opening will be shot and performed at great speed. It will be optically stylised. Main titles will be run over geographical stills of the Village and its essential components.'

Wanting something distinctive for P's transport, Everyman contacted motor manufacturers Lotus (who already provided a Lotus Elan for ABC's *The Avengers*) at Cheshunt for a possible tie-up. Home sales manager John Berry and Colin Martin-Ashwell of sales promotion met McGoohan at MGM. Lotus sales director Graham Arnold originally planned to offer an Elan for *The Prisoner*, but Graham Nearn of Caterham Cars recalled in sleeve notes for *Original Music from The Prisoner* Volume Two (Silva Screen, 1991), 'When Patrick McGoohan visited the Lotus factory […] he rejected the Lotus Elan and chose the Lotus 7 without hesitance.' The star selected the demonstrator for the Lotus Super Seven Series II 1500 range introduced in 1962; designed by Colin Chapman, the Lotus

Opposite and below:
'I know every nut and bolt and cog.' McGoohan and KAR 120C

'Be seeing you!' Barbara Yu Ling as the taxi driver.

'An elongated egg...'
The original, rejected Rover

Seven had originally been launched in kit form in 1957. Registered as KAR120C in Summer 1965, the "120" was common to all Lotus demonstrators, suggesting a top speed of 120mph. McGoohan asked for the vehicle to be repainted in British racing green with a Lotus yellow nose come. 'We needed a car for our hero,' wrote McGoohan in a Lotus brochure in 1990, 'Something out of the ordinary. A vehicle fit for his personality […] A symbol of all *The Prisoner* represented: standing out from the crowd, quickness and agility, independence and a touch of the rebel.'

In *Arrival*, the ominous Village catchphrase of "Be seeing you" was developed as a farewell expression which implied continual surveillance. The phrase had been used by Drake on various *Danger Man* episodes since *Fish on the Hook* in 1964, now introduced by a girl taxi driver who also 'gives an odd wave of the hand. It could almost be a salute.' This gesture became one with circled fingers raised to the eye. "It was the sign the Christians used to make ... the sign of the fish. That was the only thing [McGoohan] ever told me," guest star Norma West told Tony Worrall in *Number Six* Issue 4 (Summer 1985).

Another key element was Rover, a machine which disabled escapees, introduced in the second act: 'the picturesque scene is shattered by a screaming siren not unlike that of an ambulance on an errand of death […] The villagers freeze in their tracks […] the siren grows in volume. Around a corner hurtles a vehicle at great speed. It is a low-slung white Beetle-like machine. It appears to be windowless and no driver is in evidence. It looks like an elongated egg with a blue flashing police light atop. It goes to the end of the street, turns, hurtles back from where it came. Peace returns. The villagers go about their business again.'

Describing this machine as the sheepdog of his allegory, McGoohan told *New Video*, "When people start to ask too many questions or assert their individuality, the Rovers act as a stifling force. If one begins to stray from the herd, Rovers are sent out to bring them back."

McGoohan wrote his election satire, *Free For All*, in 36 hours; this looked at media manipulation as Number 6 would run for the office of Number 2 and was partly inspired by the General Election at the end of March 1966. For this script, McGoohan used the pen-name of 'Paddy Fitz', derived from the maiden-name of his mother, Rose Fitzpatrick.

With two scripts and a projected start date of late August, Everyman needed personnel. "I used the same crew that we had on [*Danger Man*]," McGoohan told Tom Soter in *Top Secret* Volume 1

Number 2 (December 1985), "They were only waiting for a phone call so I said, 'Okay, fellas, you're still in business'." Camera operator Jack Lowin and director of photography Brendan Stafford had both joined *Danger Man* in April 1964, with Stafford returning from working on the US-backed series *The Man Who Never Was*, which had been shooting in Europe since the end of May. Sound recordist John Bramall had been on *Danger Man* in November 1964, while assistant director Gino Marotta had taken over from Tomblin in October 1964 and remained to March 1965.

Young, keen Bernard Williams was made production manager, while Percy "Jack" Shampan was art director as he had been at MGM. Shampan was delighted that a McGoohan venture was moving back to MGM, but was committed to the Cliff Richard film *Finders Keepers* until mid-September. "When McGoohan first told me what he wanted in the way of mechanical wizardry, my reactions were that it couldn't be done," said Shampan in ITC publicity material, "He outlined what he had in mind and left me to work it out. That's why I didn't sleep for a week!"

Above: Production drawing by Jack Shampan.
Below, Frank Maher, doubling for McGoohan on *The Schizoid Man*

Frank Maher, the ex-Parachute Regiment stuntman of American-Irish extraction, would handle all the action material. On continuity, Doris Martin had originally joined *Danger Man* from March 1964 to July 1965, and had then taken a few months off to return in October 1965. Polish-born ATV casting director Rose Tobias Shaw, make-up artist Eddie Knight and wardrobe mistress Masada Wilmot had all been on *Danger Man* since 1964, while hairdresser Pat McDermott had left in February 1965 but returned for the colour episodes. For post-production, sound editor Wilfred Thompson had handled most episodes while film editor Lee Doig had worked on the series throughout its run. Told little about the new venture, the crew viewed it with a mixture of eagerness and apprehension, placing their faith in McGoohan.

"The head of production for ITC, Bernard Kingham, was absolutely terrified because he had to deal with McGoohan," recalled Grade's personal assistant Marcia Stanton to Robert Sellers in *Cult TV: The Golden Age of ITC*

(Plexus, 2006), "Lew said, 'Look. He's writing some of them and he's directing some of them, just let him get on with it'." As such, Kingham wanted an
experienced figure supervising the project. "I was approached by the Grade
Organisation [which was] making a thing called *The Prisoner* and they said
would I come and see them?" recalled Leslie Gilliat to Steven Ricks in *The
Prisoner on Location* (TR7 Productions, 1993). Born in 1917, Gilliat had been
in movies since the war and a film producer for some years, mainly on comedies such as *The Great St Trinian's Train Robbery* which had filmed at Shepperton from October to December 1965 alongside *Danger Man*. He had also
been a production supervisor on 1950s film series such as *Colonel March of
Scotland Yard*. Kingham outlined the series to Gilliat who was intrigued and

Above: 'You're in the hospital,
son.' McGoohan in *Arrival*.
Opposite: Filming *Checkmate*

went to meet McGoohan and Tomblin at MGM where, impressed with the two
scripts, he began as co-producer the following week.

More scripts were needed, so Markstein contacted writers to discuss
or furnish storylines for what he saw as a superior spy series. "I wasn't a script
editor, I was a story editor really," he said when interviewed for *Six into One*,
"Script editor suggests someone who blue-pencils scripts. A story editor's a man
who creates and thinks up stories." Markstein developed all the stories for the
first thirteen shows apart from those by McGoohan. McGoohan was very grateful that Markstein could locate and then wine and dine potential writers.

"We did approach some very big writers, but they said [...] why should
they work that hard for little money when they could sit at home in a warm study
and write a book for fifty times the money!" recalled Tomblin, interviewed for

*Six into One*, while McGoohan told Clifford Davis of the *Daily Mirror* (3 February 1968), "I asked one top writer to do one for us and he wanted £10,000 an episode. But we don't have that sort of budget." Using established television writers did pose a problem. "They were also prisoners of conditioning, and they were used to writing for *The Saint* or [*Danger Man*]. We lost a few by the wayside," McGoohan told Troyer. The format was tricky because Number 6 could never actually escape. "It became a sort of challenge for the writers," commented Markstein to John Dunn.

One early script was *The Queen's Pawn* by Gerald Kelsey. Kelsey started writing for television in the 1950s in partnership with Dick Sharples on A-R's juvenile adventure *Steve Hunter, Trouble Merchant*, after which the pair turned their hand to comedy with ATV's *Joan and Leslie*. The duo then worked on original scripts for *Ghost Squad* and adaptations for *The Saint*, while Kelsey regularly wrote for BBC TV's police series *Dixon of Dock Green* and ATV's *The Sullavan Brothers*. Recalling a human chess game he had seen being played while on holiday in Germany in 1959, Kelsey's script was built around the intricate strategy of the game, allied to the notion of a means of detecting which Villagers were fellow prisoners. Although Kelsey feared his submission was too "off-beat", Markstein and McGoohan were thrilled and enthusiastic about it.

On Thursday 7 July, *Television Today* announced that Anthony Skene was writing two scripts for *The Prisoner*. Born in 1924, Skene had been approached earlier in the year regarding *Danger Man*, but his script was never made. A prolific writer of radio plays for the BBC, Skene had contributed to Rediffusion's *Riviera Police* and *No Hiding Place*. He also adapted a Jean Benedetti play for Rediffusion's *Seven Deadly Sins, File on Harry Jordan*. Screened (in all areas apart from Scottish) on Monday 16 May 1966, this concerned the selection of a company employee whose private life had been scrutinised by hidden listening devices; he was now to take over the business in isolation in a room at the top of the corporation offices where he would be served by a midget butler. Heavily influenced by the 1941 film *The Devil and Daniel Webster* and Jean Cocteau's 1950 movie *Orphée*, Skene's first script – *Dance of the Dead* – saw Number 6 being declared dead to the outside world and standing a bizarre form of trial.

A fifth script, *The Chimes of Big Ben*, was developed by writer Vincent Tilsley, an Oxford history graduate who trained in ABPC's script department before becoming a story editor at the BBC. Tilsley was familiar with

McGoohan, who had appeared in his TV script *The Ruthless Destiny* on Sunday 16 October 1955. He had then adapted classics such as *David Copperfield* as BBC serials, contributed to BBC film series such as *The Third Man*, and acted as script editor of *First Night*. Tilsley was phoned by Markstein and briefed about the show with the script for *Arrival*; he then worked out a story in which Number 2 would place Number 6 in the familiar surroundings of his London office to catch him with his guard down, an idea which delighted Markstein.

From 10 July, ATV London repeated *Danger Man* on Sunday afternoons, re-running Drake's exploits through to 25 September. Around July, Grade announced that he was ideally aiming to sell around thirty episodes of *The Prisoner* to an American network, which meant McGoohan's plans for *The Prisoner* as a mini-series were soon to change. McGoohan recalled in *Top Secret* how Grade asked him to come in one Saturday morning: "He says, 'Listen, I've sold it to CBS but they'd like more.' And I said, 'I don't think we can sustain more than seven ... if you spend too long with it, you can ruin it.' So he said, 'We'd like to do twenty-six ...' I said, 'I don't know. Call me Monday morning'."

"Originally, I wanted to do only seven episodes, but CBS wouldn't buy it," recalled McGoohan in the *Washington Post* (19 November 1969). At this juncture, an attractive minimum requirement from an American network was for thirteen shows. McGoohan and Tomblin spent the weekend developing further storylines to meet this, with McGoohan calling Grade to confirm its practicality. He referred to these new ideas as padding, commenting to Alain Carrazé and Hélene Oswald in *Le Prisonnier: chef-d'oeuvre télévisionnaire* (Huitième Art, 1989): "There are seven [episodes] I consider completely true to the concept. The others on occasion were stretching it a bit."

American journalist Robert Mussel interviewed McGoohan at MGM for syndication to various US papers such as the *Desert Sun* and *New Castle News* from Monday 25 July. 'McGoohan had just crystalized the conception of his new series *The Prisoner*,' wrote Mussel, '*The Prisoner* may be one of the more gratifying TV successes of 1967 [taking] the curious world of counter-espionage into a new and dangerous dimension. It will be a one-hour show in color limited to a minimum of 13 episodes and a maximum of 30.' McGoohan bemoaned this large number of programmes: "The trouble with television is that it takes an idea and milks it to death."

"Each episode will be self-contained but part of a continuing story line," explained McGoohan to Mussel, "It will be absolutely essential, however, to see the first segment for an understanding of the series. So we are going to publish that one as a book and anyone who misses it and who is intrigued by the later episodes can get the book and read all the basic information." Of his role, McGoohan reiterated: "John Drake of *Secret Agent* is gone [...] In *The Prisoner* I've worked in a top security job and I've had enough of it so I resign. But I have a lot of secret knowledge which could be of use to the other side. So I am abducted from London and I awaken in a holiday village. It is a prison – but who is the warden? Who are the captors? Are the British trying to find out whether I am still reliable? Or is the other side trying to pump me?" McGoohan told Mussel that filming would start in Wales in September, adding: "As star and producer and even writer of some of the scripts for *The Prisoner* I'll have only myself to blame if it's a lousy show. And that's the way I like it."

Over two days around late July, Gilliat and Williams shot 16mm test footage in Portmeirion of scripted locations, assessing issues with camera positions. The first venue considered was the main hotel which became the Old People's Home. Adjacent to this was the 'Stone Boat', *Amis Reunis* (Friends Reunited), the remains of a Portmadoc ketch purchased by Williams-Ellis in 1926 and built into the quayside in 1930. The Hercules Hall, built in 1937-38 to house a Jacobean ceiling and windows salvaged from Emral Hall in Flintshire, became the Town Hall. The Salutation Italian restaurant was ideal as a cafe. Buildings in Battery Square were filmed, followed by shots of Williams running up the steps to the Unicorn (a Georgian-looking building erected in 1964) which was the intended home for Number 2. For the graveyard in *Arrival*, footage was also shot at the unused venue of Minffordd cemetery a mile away.

Shampan suggested various ideas as a Village emblem – all rejected by McGoohan. One weekend, McGoohan saw an old-fashioned penny-far-

Gilliat and Williams' original recce photograph of the hotel

Don Chaffey and Norma West try out the penny-farthing during filming on *Dance of the Dead*

thing bicycle and asked for one the following Monday. Developed in England in 1870 as the first practical bike, these were supplanted by standard bicycles after 1892. Feeling the object represented a gentler, simpler age, McGoohan explained in *Le Prisonnier*, "The ancient bicycle represented progress; one only has to be in a traffic jam for hours on the highway […] to know what that meant." As an ironic symbol of progress not making things better, McGoohan explained in 1983: "The feeling is that we are going too fast – we don't have time to assimilate as much as we should […] one has to learn quicker and quicker, because there is so much information pouring out in every direction ... I wish we could go a bit slower, but we can't." The striped canopy added to the cycle (making it impossible to ride) was "just jazz for the Village, because everything was jazzed up a little bit," he told *PrimeTime*.

The lettering used on props and series titles was a modified form of Albertus (omitting dots on 'i's and 'j's and breaking the loops of an 'e'), a font designed by Berthold Wolpe for the Monotype Corporation between 1932 and 1940, based on letters cut in bronze with a chisel.

Aside from Number 6, there was one other regular character that featured in *Arrival* but not in *Free For All*. This was Number 2's butler: 'very formal but a man in obviously good physical shape who'd be at home in an E-type Jag.' While written as a speaking part for an athletic-looking actor, the role became that of a small, mute man. Cast as the Butler was Maltese-born Angelo Muscat who stood four foot three inches. Born in September 1930, Muscat had started acting with the Maltese State Theatre Company before moving to England. Working in a factory, he heard of a requirement for small men in a touring version of *Snow White and the Seven Dwarfs* which led to television roles in *Doctor Who* and ATV's *Emergency Ward 10*; he was now represented by the Mini-People agency which specialised in reduced-stature performers. "I always feel lonely," said Muscat in ITC publicity material, "I feel that people don't want to know me. Girls don't fancy me. I'm tiny and I'm nearly bald, but I'm only in my 30s. That's why I'm so grateful to Patrick McGoohan. He has given me responsibility for the first time in my life. I'm playing an important part in a big series. I *am* something – for the first time ever. I could hardly believe it when he chose me. I have always been a fan of his and never missed a *Danger Man* episode. When he chose me, I went so red in the face I thought I was going to catch fire."

"As soon as Angelo walked in, he was the most elegant little man!" recalled McGoohan in *PrimeTime*, "He was a wonderful guy, a sweetheart of a man [...] He said, 'You've got to come out to Malta and meet me and my family out there'. So I did. I visited him there, and he had these two spanking

'The most elegant little man!'
Angelo Muscat in *Arrival*

regular-sized brothers [...] Angelo was a big man out there.
I mean big in every way! But he was so elegant! All the girls
were crazy about him!" In 1977, Markstein told Six of One,
"Angelo was a genial little man – he always had a smile on
the set at 8 o'clock in the morning and he had a marvellous
knack of being cheerful [...] One of the nicest things about
the whole series was [...] it gave Angelo a niche and a certain amount of worldwide fame."

For Village transport, Everyman arranged a tie-up
with the car manufacturers Austin to use four Mini Mokes.
The Mini Moke had been designed in 1959 by Sir Alec Issi-
gonis for the British Motor Company at the same time as his
famous Mini, of which the Moke (an archaic term for 'donkey') was a derivative, fulfilling a British Army requirement
for a lightweight off-road vehicle which could be deployed
by parachute. With front-wheel drive and an 848cc engine, the Moke was built
from January 1964 at BMC's Longbridge plant.

'A free ride home!'
Number 6 and the taxi
outside Castell Deudraeth

Further scripts were needed, and many early submissions did not fit
Everyman's vision. Markstein helped writers refine their submissions, aiming
to spend ten hours on the concept with the writer and then only ten minutes on
the script. He was pleased that none of his commissions had to be substantially
rewritten for production. McGoohan wanted something challenging, not pedestrian, as he felt *Danger Man* had become, commenting to David Gillard of the
*Radio Times* (19-25 September 1992), "If there was anything too easy in the
script, I asked for it to be changed."

A four page series format document was assembled, reading as follows:

**T.V. SERIES - WORKING TITLE " THE PRISONER "**

1. Our hero is a man who held a highly confiden-
tial job of the most secret nature. He therefore has knowledge which is invaluable or highly dangerous depending which side of the fence
he falls.

2. He resigns.

3. He is 'computerised' to the 'retired' file.

4. He is abducted from his home and transported
unconscious to a place.

5. Is he abducted by "Us" or "Them"?

6. He awakens in a village.

7. He discovers that the village is a self-contained unit of our society with its own Council of Parliament.

8. He is treated with dangerous courtesy and invited to participate in all village activity.

9. He can stand for election on the Village Council and is invited to do so.

10. He is given a cottage with maid service and every conceivable modern amenity.

But:-Every inch is bugged. His every move is watched constantly on closed circuit television.

He has to have a Security Number to warrant an issue of village currency to enable him to buy food supplies, clothing, or even a glass of beer in the village pub. In his cottage is a detailed map of the village with all exits clearly marked but they are cut off by a deadly ray barrier. Some of the residents encourage him to try and escape. Others attempt to dissuade him. They are all known by numbers, and he cannot distinguish between a possible ally and a potential enemy. Who are the Prisoners? Who are the Captors? All persons at all times behave with excessive normality against a background of sinister abnormality. They all speak English. Sometimes a foreign language is heard in distant conversation but ceases upon his approach. There are no out-going telephone calls. The Village Post Office returns all mail and cables - "Unknown".

11. Who then runs the village?

12. Is it "West" training him up to top indoc-
trination resistance?

13. "West" infiltrated by "East" trying to break
him?

14. In any event - he is a prisoner.

THE ACTION IS ON THREE LEVELS

1. Our hero constantly probes to discover why
he is a prisoner and who are his captors.

2. He strives by all means and at risk of death
to escape.

3. He becomes involved with his captors and
takes an active part in situations arising in
their lives.

BACKGROUND

1. The prison is a holiday-type village.

2. GEOGRAPHY: The village lies on a peninsula
and covers five acres. It is completely iso-
lated by a range of mountains that cut it off
from the outside on the north-west and by dense
forests on the north-east. For the rest it is
surrounded by sea. A flat beach, a mile long is
a prominent feature of the village. There are
cliffs and caves and two old mines go deep in
the bowels of the earth under the village. The
communal life of the village gravitates round
thirteen main "blocks" of buildings, villas,
bungalows, shops, etc.

3. COMMUNICATIONS: Telephone lines to the outside world are not available. There is no bus
service, no railway station, taxis do not go
outside the village. There is a closed circuit
T.V. service.

4. NAME: The village has no name. It is just the

village or "here" or "this place".

5. TRANSPORT: The village has a taxi service of mini mokes with girl drivers. There are flying strip facilities (on the beach or lawns) for helicopters to take off or land.

6. SHOPPING: The village has a tiny number of shops. The most important is the General Store which supplies everything.

7. CURRENCY: The village uses its own. There are Units which are issued in lieu of any known currency. There is also a Credit Card system.

8. THE INMATES: There are two kinds - those who have been taken there and those who run it. But we cannot necessarily tell who is who.

9. INDUSTRY: There is no single industry in the village, but the people are kept busy doing all kinds of work. There is a factory manufacturing local requisites.

10. HOSPITAL: There is a hospital which is also in actual fact a conditioning centre using the latest methods. It is situated in the Castle which stands in a clearing by itself.

11. SURVEILLANCE: Constant. Television cameras record every move and activity both indoors and outside. Every type of modern electronic surveillance system is used to keep tabs on everyone.

12. AMUSEMENTS: All catered for. There are entertainment facilities of all kinds, from chess, dancing, gambling, film shows. There is a Palace of Fun to keep 'em happy. And amateur theatricals.

13. DEATH: The village has its own graveyard.

14. KEY BUILDINGS: These include:

1. The Labour Exchange which assigns people
varied tasks, "drafts" them to wherever they
are wanted, organizes and runs the inmates.

2. The Citizen's Advice Bureau. Here all the
inmates' problems can be solved.

3. The Town Hall. The municipal office and
headquarters of the chairman.

4. The Palace of Fun.

5. The Hospital.

15. NEWSPAPER: The village produces its own.

16. T.V. - RADIO: The village has its own
units being particularly concerned with local news.

The crew were in place and the format defined. Lew Grade and ATV had made the commitment to a new and experimental project, allowing a highly regarded and globally famous actor unparalleled freedom to create a series which would be very different from the standard ITC distributed adventure fare ... and indeed very different to anything which had gone before. With two first-time producers at the help and a notion fueled by the personal vision of the lead actor, Everyman's production could begin.

# 3: "WHAT'S GOING ON HERE WITH MY TOURISTS?"

With Texan-born Richard Bradford cast as its lead, an initial thirteen episodes of *McGill* started shooting at Pinewood on Monday 15 August, with former *Danger Man* producer Sidney Cole in charge. Meanwhile, Midlands viewers got a chance to relive Drake's assignments on ATV with Friday evening reruns from 11 August to 22 September. Patrick McGoohan remained tight-lipped about his new show to the press. An interview with Ad Astra in *New Zealand TV Weekly* (1 August 1966) discussed *The Prisoner* briefly, with the star commenting merely that his character "is far removed from John Drake".

Close behind *McGill*, the first work on *The Prisoner* was the opening titles. The opening shots with stuntman Jack Cooper driving the Super Seven demonstrator straight into camera were filmed at the Santa Pod Raceway at Podington in Bedfordshire, a former RAF base which had been opened as a drag racing venue the previous Easter.

Much of the credit sequence was shot in London on Sunday 28 August. McGoohan drove the Lotus north over Westminster Bridge to the Houses of Parliament, along Margaret Street and Abingdon Street, then right into General College Street and down the ramp into Abingdon Street Car Park. The car park interior was a different venue over at Park Lane, using the barrier arm at the Cumberland Gate entrance. This location also offered the long pedestrian access corridor to Park Lane for McGoohan to walk down, and the double doors to be flung open near where the Lotus was parked. The low-roofed, impressionistic office set was built into the location. Shot mute, while striding up and down gesticulating angrily, the star recited poetry by WB Yeats, according to trainee technician F Gwynplaine MacIntyre in the *Daily Mail* (4 September 2009). Playing the man that McGoohan handed his resignation to was George Markstein, who told Roger Goodman at the ICA London on Saturday 19 April 1980 that his casting was "sheer bloody ego […] everyone wants to do a Hitchcock." In Six of One's *Alert* (Spring 1979), Markstein admitted: "I also have a yen to play a villain, but above all it seemed reasonable and fitting that, as creator of the whole fantasy, I should be the man in the centre of the web." David Tomblin felt that Markstein's bureaucratic image was right for the part, while telling *Number Six*, "But he wasn't like that at all. George was a very sweet man, a very nice man."

Other footage of the Lotus being tracked by the hearse was shot at the east end of Bayswater Road approaching Marble Arch, along Park Lane, east along the Mall and around Buckingham Palace. The Prisoner's London home was 1 Buckingham Place, positioned on the corner with Palace Street in SW1 and then owned by the Chartered Institute of Public Finance and Accountancy. Here the undertaker was played by William Lyon Brown, who had been in the *Danger Man* episode *I'm Afraid You Have The Wrong Number.* Swaying point-of-view shots of Stag Place Flats on Palace Street opposite were filmed for when P passed out.

McGoohan gets to grips with the camera on *Arrival*

Close-ups of the envelope, written in McGoohan's hand, were shot back at MGM while the character's identity photograph crossed out with 'X's was a *Danger Man* publicity shot, deposited in a filing cabinet in a set with a forced perspective painted backdrop. P's passport was actually that of second assistant director John O'Connor.

The Rover machine was a key element of exterior work for the first four episodes at Portmeirion. Working to McGoohan's guidance of a model wooden hemisphere with rings around it, assistant art director Ken Ryan produced a design to be constructed by Hillmans in Surrey. Three days before the team were due to leave for Wales, Rover was delivered to MGM. "I think his enthusiasm was stronger than his ability," Tomblin told *Number Six* of the props builder who claimed that Rover could climb walls and cross ceilings, "but then we got a go-kart which we covered with a rubber shape on it." While the prop drove around MGM's grounds perfectly, Leslie Gilliat was less convinced of its performance on the sloped, cobbled streets he had seen at Portmeirion.

For the four week shoot at Portmeirion, the crew travelled up by rail on Saturday 3 September, leaving Paddington at 11.10am and due to arrive at Portmadoc at 6.55pm. The Everyman paraphernalia was unpacked the next day in the rain. The penny-farthing prop caused great interest as Frank Maher recalled in *Number Six*: "Pat came up and said, 'Right Stuntman – ride it!' So, I tried riding it and nearly broke my neck!" To make matters worse, an onlooker asked if he could try the cycle himself, mounting the vehicle by leaning against a tree and climbing into the seat before merrily pedalling away.

Cameras and props were stored in the domed building of the Pantheon, with the Rover machine, Mokes, Bolens rider-mowers and other vehicles in a couple of garages. The production office was based at Government House. Each day, make-up for the main actors was performed in the sitting room of Chantry while wardrobe was handled at the Hercules Hall.

Many of the crew stayed in the hotel and cottages of Portmeirion itself, with others at the Queen's Hotel on Portmadoc's Station Road, the Madoc Hotel in Tremadoc, Glaslyn Hotel in Prenteg and the Woodlands Private Hotel near Portmadoc. Guest stars were generally offered rooms in the main hotel, Watch House or Fountain, while the female crew lived in Chantry. McGoohan stayed with his family in White Horses, a former workshop built just outside the village around 1830 and extended as a coastal holiday cottage months earlier. This was ideal for McGoohan's early morning runs on the beach at 5.30am each day; his wife and daughters would sometimes come and sit on the lawn to watch him filming.

Filming started on Monday 5 September with *The Arrival* (as it was now known) scheduled for the first few days to establish key locations. The Roundhouse, a baroque former cabinet maker's shop in Battery Square built around 1959, became Number 6's home. Rather than Unicorn, the Pantheon – a green plywood dome above the frontage of a huge sandstone gothic fireplace salvaged from Hooton Hall in Cheshire erected in 1959 – became Number 2's house. Red and white striped screens hid cars and other non-Village items, while smaller objects could be obscured by a penny-farthing logo. Portmeirion was still in use by the public, with signs and assistant directors managing tourists to allow shooting to proceed.

It was decided that the different Number 2s would have shooting stick umbrellas crafted at Smiths of New Oxford Street. Costumes came from Berman's in London, while John Michael of London furnished the eye-catching blazer that McGoohan would sport as Number 6. Village garb was specifically designed to be ageless, meaning that the look of the series would not date quickly. Props man Mickey O'Toole had fun at the expense of costume assistant Catherine Williams when she asked about the costume Angelo Muscat would require, telling her that he was "a great big lad"; this resulted in the Butler's outdoor wear being hastily fashioned from a black donkey jacket.

Filming with the *Danger Man* star generated a lot of local interest. Extras included a headmaster, labourers,

Guy Doleman with his shooting stick umbrella, on location for *Arrival*

41

office workers and a shorthand typist who phoned up from 200 miles away. Jonathan Jones was recruited at Portmadoc Labour Exchange to organise 95 extras, and found that *everyone* wanted to join in. "Amongst the extras there were two brothers who were meths drinkers," recalled Jones to Max Hora in *Portmeirion Prisoner Production* (Number Six, 1985), "They were very popular with McGoohan. He liked characters you see." It was these brothers that Samuel Owen Hughes recalled to Arabella McIntyre-Brown in *The Tally Ho* (October 1987): "One day, one of them was standing in an odd way, sort of half-leaning because he was drunk, and McGoohan saw him and said, 'That's the way I want everyone to stand still when Rover goes past." The crowd artists were paid £2 10s at the end of each day in the Hercules Hall.

Filming was rapid and tightly controlled. Schedules were amended daily as the crew struggled to capture McGoohan's vision. Maher recalled only two complete scripts were available along with location sequences of others, and during September some exterior sections of *The Chimes of Big Ben* arrived, having been completed in late August. Generally two units were at work: Don

These pages: 'There's not a lot to do at Portmeirion...'

Chaffey's main unit shot key dialogue scenes while a second unit covered establishing shots, cutaway inserts, and work with stand-ins for the main cast. Although the hours were generally 8am to 10pm, the unit was generally a happy one. However, the crew did feel somewhat imprisoned. As Maher observed on BBC Radio 5's *Cult Radio* (27 July 1993), "There's not a lot to do at Portmeirion after two or three days."

Tomblin had arranged with Paramount Pictures for five to eight minutes of silent rushes from the previous day to be projected by Bob Piercy at the Coliseum Cinema in Portmadoc each night around 10pm after the evening's programme. Each day, raw film was taxied to Bangor, shipped to London by rail, then collected again from Bangor next day.

On Tuesday 6 September it was planned to shoot the sequence introducing

Rover by the main hotel. The prop was successfully tested in the car park at the 1840s structure of Castle Deudraeth (purchased by Williams-Ellis in 1931), but problems then became apparent. The cobbled street caused steering problems, and the two-stroke petrol engine was noisy. Visibility through a small hole for the operator was poor, but if this panel was enlarged the driver inside would be seen. Chaffey and the crew were unimpressed by the heavy domed prop which was battered even before shooting began. Despite reservations, Bernard Williams took his place at the wheel beneath the dome. "I nearly died," he said in Radio 4's *Britain in a Box* (17 July 2004), "I couldn't see. I had this little [viewing] slit and now I'm breathing in car fumes. And I got out and said, 'This is totally ridiculous! Forget it!'"

If Rover on land caused problems, its sea variant was even worse. "This thing was like a hovercraft and it would go underwater, come up on the beach, climb walls … it could do anything," McGoohan told Warner Troyer, "And the first day of shooting, Rover was supposed to go down off the beach into the water, do a couple of signals and a couple of wheel spins and come back up. But it went down into the water and stayed down, permanently."

"In desperation, Bernard Williams and myself were standing there in the village," McGoohan recounted in 1983, "We were looking up in agony at the heavens, and we saw this white thing, way up there in the blue. He said it must be

a meteorological balloon. I said, 'Do you think that thing could do? What size is it? Find out ...' He took off like a rocket [and] arrived back with a station wagon full of these balloons."

However, Chaffey related a different story when interviewed for *Six into One*, recalling problems he was having at the time dealing with GPO officials about installing a telephone in his squash court. "'We have to remain anonymous, we're civil servants!'," Chaffey was told, "I said: 'No, what you bloody well are are a lot of white balloons!' Then I went away and thought, 'White balloons! My God!' and I jumped on the phone to Pat." A third story was that second unit camera operator Ronnie Fox-Rogers pointed out the bubbles in an oil-based Astro lamp to McGoohan in Portmeirion's bar; this was later used for the back projection image frequently seen in Number 2's office and the shot of Rover being created on the ocean floor.

A panic call was put into props buyer Sidney Palmer back at MGM. Palmer initially considered solid balls – akin to those used by the Metropolitan Police horses as footballs at the Horse of the Year Show – as replacements, but then recalled fulfilling a previous requirement for large beach balls of all sizes via a company in the Midlands. The off-white Air Ministry weather balloons ranged from six inches to eight feet in diameter; they were inflated with a mixture of helium and oxygen to make them bounce plus a bit of water to weigh them down. Mickey O'Toole suggested moving the balloons using fine fishing wire tied to their quarry. Filled with French chalk, the balloons were delicate, and the crew inflated a continual supply of them as many burst before even reaching the set. Others simply blew away, with local Tecwyn Williams given the job of recovering escapees after the coastguards arrived to enquire why so many large white balloons had been spotted at sea. The hasty replacement was perfect for McGoohan who commented in *Le Prisonnier*, "The balloon represented the greatest fear of all – the Unknown."

Above: 'The greatest fear of all...' McGoohan with Rover. Opposite: McGoohan chooses a buggy to study his script

Rover also had to be aquatic. "Patrick – have you ever blown a balloon up under the water?" asked Williams, recalling events in *Britain in a Box*, and receiving the answer, "Go figure it out – shoot it – just get it done." Local diver Brain Axworthy helped inflate the Rovers with compressed air borrowed from an RAF base. The sequences of Rover surfacing were filmed by underwater cameraman Ronnie Fox-Rogers in the deeper waters of Llyn Cwm Bychan in Llanbedr where the balloons were held down with nets and cement blocks.

The plan had been to complete most exteriors for *The Arrival* by Friday 9 September and then start on *Free For All* the next day, but the shoot was behind schedule. Chaffey was still filming the debut episode through to Sunday 18, with some material for *Dance of the Dead* filmed as early as Tuesday

6 as the schedule changed. Further title sequence material was also filmed. An early version of this described as 'Standard Opening and Link: Episode 2 and thereafter' appeared on the scripts for *Free For All, Dance of the Dead, The Chimes of Big Ben* plus subsequent entries such as *The Schizoid Man* and *It's Your Funeral*. The first main title appeared at the window shot, after which P turned to look at his room ('Same divan, same carpet, same wall-paper') and then rushed out into the street; from above, a panoramic shot zoomed in on his tiny lonely figure asking "Where am I?" The camera zoomed in through the window to a wall speaker which nonchalantly replied, "In the village," as the second title appeared. P was then on a deserted balcony, a statue swivelling to face him as he asked, "What do you want?" "Information", the voice gently replied as the third title appeared. Running away along the beach, P shouted, "You won't get it," as the fourth title appeared; this shot in turn was shown on one of many monitors watched by a silhouetted figure who rebukingly stated, "We will." "I'm a free man," bellowed P on the beach as a thunderclap rang through the sunny day and the fifth title appeared. Next came a cut to 'the winking blue light of "Rover"', herding P back along the beach. As the camera zoomed in on P's face, gates clanged shut across it and his features diminished into a speck beyond the prison bars as the sixth and final title appeared.

It had been hoped to shoot the beach material for these titles on Sunday 11 September, but these were deferred to Thursday 15, and finally seem

Mingling with the locals during filming on *Free For All* and, below, extras in village garb on location in Portmeirion.

to have been filmed on Sunday 18. Maher performed the iconic shots of Number 6 running and punching the air defiantly. "Patrick tried to do it himself, but fell over and pulled a muscle," said the stuntman, recalling the problems of running on sand to Pat Small in *East Anglian Daily Times* (21 January 1993).

McGoohan himself was working sixteen-hour days, attempting a high throughput with up to 27 set-ups a day. Nevertheless, production secretary Tina Davies recalled that McGoohan was always polite and found time to speak to people. The pressure on him was evident as she told Dave Jones in Six of One's fanzine *In the Village* Issue 14 (Spring 1997), recalling how she told McGoohan in the bar one night: "Everyone's worried about you, because you're working too hard and without you there wouldn't be a series." The star put his hand on her shoulder and said, "Don't worry about me." Jonathan Jones commented in *Portmeirion Prisoner Production*, that "Patrick McGoohan was a bit distant until you got used to him […] However, if you got him on his own he had quite a lot to say." Speaking to Emyr Williams in the *Daily Post* (14 June 1999), local extra Brenda Owen recalled, "McGoohan was so ordinary and I remember him queuing up with local people at the fish and chip shop [in Snowdon Street] in Portmadoc. He was so down-to-earth and hated people calling him 'Sir'." In comparison with his time on *Danger Man*, Maher realised that McGoohan was now a harder taskmaster, exhibiting the ultimate in professionalism and expecting those around him to do the same. In *Number Six*, he recalled "Pat would say something once and expect you to accept it if you understood it […] Once you walked away from him you didn't come back and ask the same question again – because if you did he'd flip his lid!"

Clough Williams-Ellis' reaction to the crew was mixed. In the revised edition of his book *Portmeirion: The Place and its Meaning* (Portmeirion, 1973), Clough wrote 'McGoohan took the greatest trouble to cause the minimum of disturbance of the place's normal life by his large cast. I certainly appreciated his care.' McGoohan would occasionally take evening dinner with the proprietor to ensure good relations. During the day, Williams-Ellis would hover around on the edge of filming, occasionally suggesting a suitable location. Although daily call sheets stressed 'PLEASE KEEP PORTMEIRION

TIDY', the owner would still be seen clearing up after the team as he did with the daily visitors. Portmeirion still housed other guests not connected with Everyman, as Bernard Williams remembered on *Britain in a Box*: "Clough Williams-Ellis would come down and say, 'What's going on here with my tourists?' 'Nothing sir, nothing. We'll take care of it. We'll send them some flowers and some fruit in a bowl'."

"There were rather mixed feelings here," said Portmeirion hotel manager Trevor Williams in *TV Times* (28 October–3 November 1967), "All those under 50 welcomed the television people and thought it was great. Those over 50 regarded them as intruders." One of the deals that Williams-Ellis had made with Everyman Films was that Portmeirion would *not* be revealed as the Village until the final instalment. However, the press were soon onto the new series, with one paper running the story *Hush – He's in Danger Again* and giving readers a first glimpse of the blazered star. "No one really wants you to know, but *Danger Man* Patrick McGoohan is shooting a television film in North Wales. Here he is being hotly pursued as usual. Says the TV company: 'The owner of the location is only allowing us to use it on condition that no publicity is given out.'"

On Wednesday 14 September, the helicopter needed for both aerial shots and action scenes in *The Arrival, Free For All* and *The Chimes of Big Ben* arrived for two day's work. This was a French-made SE-3130 Alouette II (meaning 'Lark'), manufactured by Sud-Aviation from 1955. This Alouette, F-BNKZ, was owned by Héli-Union, and in August had been used for *Roundabout*, an episode of *The Baron*. The 32 foot long five-seater gas turbine craft was flown by an ex-RAF pilot called Charles James. Decked out with penny-farthing markings to obscure its true identification, the helicopter was used over three days, with the second unit taking to the air to capture aerial shots of the Village (often revealing non-Village vehicles, like a black car parked behind the Pantheon). In the *TV Times* (28 October-3 November 1967), Williams-Ellis' secretary Mary Roberts commented that "The helicopter caused quite a stir and brought the locals out to see what was going on."

Meanwhile, *The Prisoner* was covered by Tony Gruner's *Television* column in *Kinematograph Weekly* (15 September 1966). Under the title, *Is McGoohan making a modern morality play?*, Gruner asked, 'Who is making the most intriguing tv series in Britain today? None other than Patrick McGoohan, the John Drake of *Danger Man*.' The journalist explained that the star of the 'new one-hour film series in colour' had devised the show and enjoyed 'complete artistic control' as executive producer of this 'entirely new type of British series' which 'has nothing in common with anything that ITC or McGoohan

Filming *Dance of the Dead* and, opposite, *Free For All*

has ever done before.' Noting that 'some of the writers engaged [...] can't understand all its ramifications,' Gruner reported that the show had a 'futuristic basis within the format of mystery and intrigue'. One writer claimed it was 'a modern morality story dealing with the striving of people for a better life.' The format featured 'a *Danger Man* character' who wanted to leave the espionage world. 'One day the head of department agrees and the hero goes back to his flat intending to go on a long and well-earned sabbatical.' One person who had read the pilot script described it (in reference to the successful American series then running on ITV) as 'a sort of British *Fugitive*', while another felt it was akin to the 1965 espionage film *The Spy Who Came in from the Cold,* and a third drew comparisons with Kafka's *The Trial*. 'One writer believes [it] is about the contemporary rat-race. Another told me *The Prisoner* was the most way-out programme he has ever written for.' It was indicated that McGoohan was going in for a lot of the technical gimmicks and gadgets which made *Danger Man* so popular. Furthermore, he was taking a personal interest in the scripts, sets and casting. When he returned to MGM in three weeks' time, McGoohan would begin twelve months of work on a show that was not due to air on British screens until Autumn 1967. Gruner noted that this long lead time led to fears that some of the star's unusual ideas might be poached by American producers and a lot of secrecy: 'Only a few people apparently know what is going on and they're saying little at the present time – and certainly nothing without reference to McGoohan.'

Meanwhile, filming at Portmeirion moved on to *Free For All*. For the third week, camera operator Jack Lowin arrived and was amazed by the location. Exteriors for *The Queen's Pawn* were scheduled from Saturday 17 and occupied much of the third week, actually starting on Monday 19. During this shoot, McGoohan swapped his original blazer (with unbroken piping) for a new one (with broken piping); apart from a couple of studio inserts, the original was not used again. The original schedule for Thursday 22 September was set aside for the sea sequences with the raft and the vessel the *MS Polotska*, using the local motor yacht *Breda* from Portmadoc for filming over two days at Abersoch, some way west along the Welsh coast.

Back in London, Lew Grade was preparing to take *The Prisoner* across the Atlantic. On Friday 23 September, the *Daily Express* reported that the ATV executive was to fly to the US the following week to sell six million pounds' worth of show: 'The new plans hinge on a Patrick McGoohan series called *The Prisoner* which is now in production.'

*Dance of the Dead* was the main episode lined up for the fourth week, originally planned for filming on Friday 23, Monday 26 and Tuesday 27 September. Material for *The Chimes of Big Ben* in the form of establishing shots could then be fitted in. The good weather held through to the last day, Friday 30 September, when McGoohan (who had taken over as director mid-week while Chaffey returned to MGM to prepare for studio work) dashed around Portmeirion with a handheld camera cramming in all manner of last minute shots including Number 6's first encounter with Rover for

*The Arrival*. Everyman paid for a wrap party at the Glaslyn Hotel attended by crew and local extras, although McGoohan was conspicuous by his absence.

Gilliat was uneasy during the shoot. "I had a reputation for bringing out films under budget and on schedule. I didn't want to get involved with something that was going off the rails," he explained in *The Prisoner on Location*. The producer was concerned about escalating costs and McGoohan's inability to offer a clear conclusion. "I think he wanted a free hand," explained Gilliat, "So I wished him the best of luck and retired gracefully." Bernard Williams opined on *Don't Knock Yourself Out* that Gilliat was "too cynical, sceptical about the whole show." Trade magazines still listed Gilliat and Tomblin as co-producers through to mid-November. With the experienced producer gone, more financial duties fell on McGoohan who, talking to Roger Goodman in April 1979, admitted, "It's not really my role at all […] Monetary things are absolutely outside my field."

The crew departed from Portmeirion on Saturday 1 October. The same day, another article on the series appeared in Radio Luxembourg's magazine *Fabulous 208*. Around now, one anonymous crew member told Tony Gruner of *Kinematograph Weekly* (10 February 1968), "This show will be either the biggest flop in the history of British television or its greatest success."

Interior shooting at MGM began with *The Arrival* on Monday 3 October. The production generally filmed on Stages 6 and 7, also using Stages 4 and 5, and it was hoped to complete a show to the standard ITC two-week turnaround. On Tuesday 4, McGoohan wrote to Clough Williams-Ellis, 'Please forgive my mental and physical fatigue of Saturday evening. Any lack of enthusiasm was not for want of appreciation of your beautiful home.' The architect had been keen to see the location footage, but the star persuaded him that 'it would be fairer to both of us if we complete an entire episode [...] so that you could get an overall impression of what we are about,' and closed, 'Once again, our profound thanks for your patience and gracious forbearance in very trying circumstances.'

The first script described Number 6's home as 'spacious. Beautifully laid out as was his own London home. There is one window. The front door and another [...] Behind it a luxurious bathroom. [P] returns to the principal living area. Opens various built-in doors. The first reveals a wardrobe – empty. The second – a chest of drawers [...] The third – an expanding unit desk [...] The next built-in door reveals a compact kitchenette.' This interior, created for the title sequence, had a couple of changes for its appearance in the Village; notably, a wall panel above the sofa on which Number 6 passed out vanished to be replaced by an ornate window, mirroring the Portmeirion exterior. The backdrop behind the front door showed Government House and Dolphin, while the Gloriette and Salutation could be seen on a similar painting through the window.

Above, top: 'Welcome to your home from home.'
Below: The 'Living Space'

Number 2 was indicated as inhabiting the 'Living Space [...] a highly-stylised set. Futuristic. There is a feeling of vast, almost unending space. In the centre at a half-moon desk we see Number 2 [...] There is no other furniture.' This vast circular set was constructed over a tank, containing a troublesome underfloor mechanism that allowed various chairs and tables to emerge from beneath and which often had to be attended by Jack Shampan. Mounted on a rotating dais was a ball chair devised in 1963 by Finnish designer Eero Aarnio as "a room within a room". Looking for imported contemporary furniture, Sidney Palmer acquired the first of these prototypes in the UK from a prop firm. Ignoring his hire agreement, he took a cast of the chair and copied it for subsequent production, for which he ended up paying a fine. The hemisphere of the Living Space also appeared as numerous other sets (e.g. the Labour Exchange Manager's office in *The Arrival*), featuring mainly as the Control Room in which the dais supported a strange see-saw monitor device that caused endless problems. Generally, scenes in Number 2's Living Space and the Control Room were left until the end of the filming schedule because they frequently required the back projection of footage shot on other sets onto its huge back projection screen; this caused problems as there was not enough throw to generate an image large enough, something which Shampan solved by reflecting the projected material into an optical mirror and back onto the screen. Much of the interior illumination in the Village came from Astro lamps (or Lava lamps), devices creating swirling shapes of heated wax developed by Craven Walker in 1963.

Joining the cast for *The Arrival* was Peter Swanwick who would become a regular face on the show as the Supervisor, Number 28. Born in Nottingham in 1922, Swanwick had been acting since 1947 and had appeared in two episodes of *Danger Man*: *The Key* in 1959 and *The Paper Chase*. "He said at the time the series was made that it was far before its time, and that people would not understand what *The Prisoner* was trying to say," said Swanwick's widow, Nellie, in *Number Six* Issue 4 (Spring 1995).

McGoohan worked longer hours than ever. "[Pat and I] used to go out and play an hour's squash every night after shooting, then had a few jars, so it was usually ten o'clock before we got home," recalled Maher on *Cult Radio*, while in *In the Village* Issue 15 (Summer 1997), Jack Lowin told Dave Jones: "He used to go to bed at around midnight and at about 3 o'clock he would get up again and write all his letters and do his correspondence, or write some scripts [...] go back to bed for about another hour and be in the studio again at about 7 o'clock."

In studio, McGoohan asked the crew to experiment with new lighting techniques and eye-catching ways of filming. He offered off-beat casting ideas while non-speaking crowd artists were supplied by Central Casting (UK) Limited. George Markstein was seldom seen on set, staying in his office working on scripts.

The different working methods of McGoohan and Chaffey caused friction when production fell behind schedule. "A man must create pressure in his working life, something to which he can respond and must overcome," commented McGoohan in *TV World* (25 November-1 December 1967). "I have sometimes been accused of being difficult and edgy and complicated. This is only because I want the end product to be as perfect as possible. I haven't always endeared myself to some people."

On Wednesday 5 October, *Variety* reported that Lew Grade and his assistant Robin Gill were in the US for the week aiming to place *The Prisoner* off the back of *Secret Agent*'s success. Grade approached CBS station founder William Paley and Grade's friend Michael Dann, the channel's Senior

An early Astro Lamp illustrated in a US catalogue
Below: 'Orange alert!' Peter Swanwick as Number 28

51

Vice President of Programming, knowing that as well as *Danger Man* the network had purchased *The Adventures of Robin Hood* back in 1955. "They asked me if I had any fresh series ideas. I told them I had a project called *The Prisoner* with Patrick McGoohan, and showed them a portfolio of pictures of the village of Portmeirion […] 'How much money do you want?' they asked. I told them the terms and they said we had a deal," recalled Grade in his autobiography *Still Dancing: My Story* (William Collins, 1987). "He gave me this script […] and I read it, and had no concept of the scope of it," Dann told Carl Weiner in *Number Six* Issue 7 (Spring 1986), "Lew told me McGoohan had spent his life thinking about this concept ... and was devoted to it." Dann was excited by the series, but concerned the hero Number 6 would emerge as a loser each week …

On Monday 10 October, Grade announced the success of his trip to America. *It's a Dollar Jackpot for ATV* was the *Daily Mirror*'s headline the next day as the seven million dollars of business was reported to include the sale of *The Prisoner* to CBS for screening concurrent with ITV in September 1967. In *The Guardian*, Richard Milner enthusiastically claimed that this was 'the first time a British series has been bought for the start of a TV season.' In *Variety* on Wednesday 12, Grade was quoted as saying: "I couldn't tell you about *The Prisoner*. All the London newspapers would like to know what Patrick McGoohan will be up to in *The Prisoner*. [The series] may range in cost from $155,000 to $180,000 we'll have the equivalent of $400,000 on the screen if it was made in Hollywood." These reports also confirmed that CBS' order was for a minimum of seventeen shows – four more than the Everyman team had been planning. The trade magazine *Broadcast* (24 October 1966) covered the network sale of *The Prisoner* for a couple of screenings. However, Grade's deal was only $120,000 per episode, not the $150,000 he wanted.

Although it had originally been planned to shoot the interiors for *The Queen's Pawn* from around Thursday 20 October, the next episode onto the sound stages was *Free For All*, for which McGoohan himself took over directing from Chaffey; this was reported in the Friday 21 and 28 October editions of the *Daily Cinema*, by which time the drama *Stranger in the House* had moved into the adjoining sound stages. For *Free For All*, the Living Space set also doubled as the Council Chamber, complete with revolving platform. *The Queen's Pawn* was then reported as shooting at MGM on Wednesday 2 and Wednesday 9 November. By this time, the standing Living Space set was starting to show signs of wear as the silver covering around the entrance door began to bubble and distort.

Episodes now started to be assembled with Geoff Foot, who had edited for David Lean, setting a visual style for the series alongside Lee Doig; the editors were assisted by Eric Mival and Harry Macdonald respectively. Tony Sloman joined as the film librarian to track all the material required to make finished programmes. Stock footage generally came from local company World Backgrounds run by Ralph Rogers, while sound effects (including the

'Who elected you?' Number 6 in the Council Chamber in *Free For All*

distinctive thunderclap which opened the title sequence) were furnished by sound editor Wilfred Thompson's company Cinesound. One of Thompson's first audio creations was Rover, effectively the breathing of a deep sea diver combined with a mechanised heartbeat. Many of the male voices added in post-production were supplied by actor Robert Rietty, whom McGoohan remembered directing as a Russian translator in the *Danger Man* episode *To Our Best Friend* a year earlier; while female voices were often those of Olive Gregg.

The *Daily Cinema* listed *Dance of the Dead* as filming for the week of Wednesday 16 November; by now, damage to the Living Space (also seen in this episode as the Town Hall Ball Room) had been repaired by the addition of metal struts across the distorted door frame.

With *Danger Man* off the air, fans of McGoohan wrote to him, eager for news of his new show. 'Currently, I am engaged in preparation for a new Series entitled *The Prisoner* which we hope will be with you some time in September '67,' the star replied, 'If you care for prior information on this, please write to me at the above address and I shall be delighted to oblige. Kind regards, Cordially, Patrick McGoohan.'

## 4: "I KNEW PAT WAS GOING TO HATE IT"

By late November 1966, *The Chimes of Big Ben* was filming. With only a few scenes shot at Portmeirion, new exteriors had to be undertaken on the backlots of MGM where the film *Battle Beneath the Earth* had started shooting on Monday 14 November. Because of its lack of location work, *The Chimes of Big Ben* saw the first major use of the mock-up replica sets of Portmeirion in the soundstages. The lot representing the Village comprised a large courtyard area, a twin-tunnelled building and a large hall resembling the entrance to a Norman church, which had been constructed for *Eye of the Devil* in November 1965. Pick-ups with doubles for the episode's raft sequences were shot at The Warren and Copt Point along the coast near Folkestone in Kent.

Appearing as Number 2 in *The Chimes of Big Ben* was Australian actor Leo McKern. Don Chaffey had previously worked with McKern on projects such as the Disney venture *The Horse Without a Head* (filmed from April 1962) and *A Jolly Bad Fellow* (shot in 1963). Interviewed for the DVD release of the film *The Day the Earth Caught Fire* (Network, August 2001), McKern recalled his first meeting with Patrick McGoohan: "He called me, 'You're a funny little fucker aren't you?' And I thought, 'It's going to be that sort of a relationship!' That was said in a bar before we started."

*The Chimes of Big Ben* was the last episode directed by Don Chaffey. "I understand that he finally had a quarrel with Pat," said Sidney Cole in a conversation for the BECTU History Project in August 1988. After completing post-production on his instalments, Chaffey moved on to direct an episode of *Man in a Suitcase* (the new title for *McGill* since September) in February 1967. "There were some bitter arguments," he said when interviewed for *Six into One*, "[but] out of it came what I think is one of the best television series ever made."

While Tony Sloman continued to log the footage, there was still no finished episode in sight. The first composer considered for the series was Edwin Astley who had scored *Danger Man*. "I went over to MGM a couple of times to see [McGoohan] but the trouble was he was so involved," Astley told Vanessa Bergman in RAHDAS Newsletter No 3 (Spring 1990), "We never really got down to serious talk about it, so I couldn't really get out what he was driving at […] I was very busy at the time on [*The Saint*] so I just let it go."

Merchandise for the series was being considered with a feature in the December 1966 issue of trade magazine *British Toys*. The 'great follow-up to *Danger Man*' was said to have 'a futuristic feel' and concerned 'a *Danger Man* character who quits the secret service business because he is fed up with the rat race […]

Having read the first script we found the series utterly fascinating and exciting. We feel this could well be the BIG live action drama series of 1967.' Marketing was handled by Century 21 Merchandising, another company within the ATV empire formed around the Supermarionation series such as *Thunderbirds*. Their plans for *The Prisoner* included books, a comic strip (possibly for the Supermarionation-heavy *TV Century 21* which was sent the first script for consideration) and an action figure of Number 6. "I'm not going to be turned into a dolly or a comic strip!" was apparently McGoohan's reaction to these proposals put forward by merchandising manager Richard Culley.

Impressed with McKern in *The Chimes of Big Ben*, McGoohan quickly wrote (in another 36 hour frenzy) a two-hander for the actor and himself under the title *Degree Absolute*; this was a cost-conscious and intense confrontation between Number 6 and Number 2. With no other scripts available, *Degree Absolute* was rushed into studio although not entirely finished. The *Daily Cin-*

*ema* for Wednesday 7 December noted 'Patrick McGoohan currently directing *Degree Absolute*'. To help get this bizarre, extreme script past the crew, Mc-Goohan had a plan. "I hadn't put my name on it," he explained in 1983, "I used to write under pseudonyms – one was Archibald Schwartz, which is a splendid Irish name [...] Everyone thought it was a crazy, ridiculous script." George Markstein felt the script was gibberish and had little to do with it.

'Till death do us part...' Above and opposite, Leo McKern returns to the role of Number 2 in *Once upon a Time*

Although shot sixth, McGoohan maintained that he always saw this episode as the first half of a two-part conclusion to the series which would be shelved and shown at the end of the run. The crew recalled that *Degree Absolute* would go out at the end of the first series if *The Prisoner* was screened in an initial batch of thirteen shows.

The intensity of *Degree Absolute* took its toll on McKern, who recalled on *The Day the Earth Caught Fire*: "I used to get very depressed [lying] in my dressing room in the short times we had off and worry and be depressed and very silent [...] The person inside is very withdrawn and very quiet [...] Certainly when one is shouted at it doesn't inspire one to do anything except withdraw into oneself."

Speaking to Warner Troyer, McGoohan explained, "Leo, one lunch-time, went up to his dressing room and I went to see the rushes and I knew he was tired. I went up to the dressing room to tell him how good I thought he'd been [...] And he was curled up in the foetus position on his couch [saying] 'Go away! Go away you bastard! I don't want to see you again […] I've just ordered two doctors […] and they're coming over as soon as they can.' […] He'd truly cracked. And so I had to use a double [but] eventually Leo did come back."

Interviewed for *The Prisoner Behind the Scenes* (A&E, 2000) Bernard Williams recalled, "Leo McKern got into a serious heart problem, it got so intense that we had to stop filming and we had to get Leo off the set." McKern was away from the sound stages for several days, but returned later for pick-ups. Mickey O'Toole recalled on *The Prisoner Investigated* (TR7 Productions, 1990) that when he met McKern years later and reminded him of *Degree Absolute*, the actor said, "Don't mention that. I was demented. I didn't know what I was doing."

While waiting for McKern's return, work began on the next episode, *The Schizoid Man*, a script written within two weeks by Terence Feely. Born in Liverpool in 1928, former journalist Feely had written for series such as *The Avengers* and *No Hiding Place* (edited by Markstein) and the off-beat 1964 stage play *Don't Let Summer Come*, which caught Markstein's attention when performed at the Mermaid Theatre. Feely was then working as an ABC story editor on series like *Armchair Theatre* and in 1966 had been trying to get a movie project off the ground with McGoohan. Intrigued by the new series, Feely offered Markstein an idea in which Number 2 attempted to crack Number 6 by confronting him with a double who had been programmed to believe that he was the real Number 6; this was partly inspired by the fact that Feely himself had heard that he had a double living in Germany.

Direction of *The Schizoid Man* was offered by McGoohan to his old colleague Pat Jackson. Born in Eltham in 1916, Jackson had been in films since the 1930s, making short documentaries, and had directed movies since the war. Impressed with McGoohan in Orson Welles' *Moby Dick Rehearsed* at the Duke of York Theatre in June 1955, he had invited the actor to Pinewood for a screen test, casting him in two episodes of the film anthology *Rendezvous* in 1959. Jackson had directed the *Danger Man* episode *The Hunting Party* in December 1965 and more recently helmed the debut and subsequent instalments of *Man in a Suitcase*.

Jackson was thrilled with his first script which was in production from mid-December through to the start of January 1967, concurrent with pick-ups

'Physical advantage of growing a moustache overnight!' McGoohan in *The Schizoid Man*. Below: Jack Shampan's Christmas card

for *Degree Absolute*; it was listed in the *Daily Cinema* for Wednesday 14 and Wednesday 21 December as well as Wednesday 4 January 1967. For exterior shooting on the backlot, the Alouette used at Portmeirion was not available and so a similar model, F-BOEH registered in November 1966, was supplied by Héli-Union. Although it had been planned for the vehicle to fly across the Channel, poor winter weather forced it to arrive on a trailer.

With ATV keen to see a finished episode, the pressure on McGoohan was enormous. As well as producing, directing and acting, McGoohan now also supervised the editing. The objective was that each show should run to just over 48 minutes across six reels of 35mm film. Lee Doig had assembled a rough version of *Arrival* (as the episode was now renamed). Spencer Reeve joined the editing team for *The Chimes of Big Ben*, and with him brought Robert Dearberg as music editor. To score the series, the crew turned to Robert Farnon, a Canadian percussionist and leading exponent of light orchestral music. At MGM, Farnon met McGoohan who asked for theme music like Jerome Moross' composition for the 1958 Western *The Big Country* to match Geoff Foot's edited title sequence.

Farnon's theme was recorded at Anvil Studios in Denham on the evening of Monday 19 December. Dearberg listened in horror as the tune was effectively a variation on *The Big Country* with violins against an insistent drumbeat. "I knew Pat was going to hate it," said Dearberg to Steven Ricks on *The Prisoner In-Depth* Tape 6 (TR7 Productions, 1994). Next day, Farnon recorded his incidental score for *Arrival* for which he used a lot of percussive jazz, inspired by Henry Mancini's score for the 1958 American detective show *Peter Gunn*. McGoohan rejected the theme, and a few weeks later Farnon reworked it for the new ITC/Scoton series *The Champions* (which was to shoot at ABPC from Monday 6 February); ultimately, this too was unused.

At short notice, the Everyman team approached avant-garde musician Wilfred Josephs whom Chaffey had worked with on the film *Lies My Father Told Me* in 1960. Invited to MGM by Chaffey, Josephs got on well with McGoohan who shared his outlandish nature. This time, McGoohan's brief was an incongruous mixture of Malvina Reynold's 1962 song *Little Boxes* (which lampooned suburban conformity) and Ludwig van Beethoven's 1824 composition *Symphony No 9: Choral*. Josephs drafted a theme which he felt was exciting and sinister on Thursday 22 December.

Jack Shampan designed a crew Christmas card; this featured an eye shape, within which a puzzled Butler was looking at gift-wrapped penny-farthing with a label reading 'Best wishes for 1967'. Shooting continued on Christmas Eve with pick-ups on *The Queen's Pawn* directed by McGoohan. According to one account, Markstein woke on Christmas Day and realised that he was probably supposed to be at work, turning up to find McGoohan sitting alone on the sound stage. "George, on my birthday, everyone has a day off!" said the star.

Conducted by Philip Martel, Josephs' theme and score for *Arrival* were recorded at Denham on Monday 2 January 1967, deferred from Wednesday 28 December. The theme opened with timpani effects for the Westminster Bridge shots and then *Holiday for Drums* as Number 6 strode down the corridor. For incidentals, Josephs introduced themes for Number 6, an eerie motif for Number 2's office, a harpsichord for the Supervisor and an oboe for Rover. While Chaffey liked the cues, Josephs was un-nerved by two silent, hard-faced men who sat at the back of the studio.

The build-up to *The Prisoner* was carefully planned months before its debut by ATV Midlands. In early January, *Danger Man* repeats were scheduled for Thursday nights from 5 January to run right through to the autumn on 22 September.

At MGM, things were tense for filming on Michael Cramoy's script *It's Your Funeral*, a thriller about disinformation concerning an assassination attempt on a departing Number 2 by his successor. Cramoy came to prominence writing adventure scripts in America in the 1940s, including editions of *The Saint* on radio and *Highway Patrol* and *Dragnet* on television. He came to England in 1957 to work on British film series such as ITP's *H.G. Wells' Invisible Man* and had subsequently written for *The Saint* and *The Baron*.

Directing *It's Your Funeral* was Robert Asher. Born in 1915, Asher's career in movies had predominantly been comedies featuring Norman Wisdom and more recently the film debut of Eric Morecambe and Ernie Wise. He had also directed on *The Baron* since April 1966, then *To Kill a Saint* for *The Saint* in December. According to guest star Annette Andre, talking to Robert Fairclough in *The Prisoner: the official companion to the classic TV series* (Carlton Books, 2002), "[Asher] was a friend of Patrick's, and Patrick had insisted that he come and direct that episode and more if possible."

*It's Your Funeral* was listed in the MGM production schedules on Wednesday 11 and Wednesday 18 January. While Asher was the director, Mc-Goohan was very hands on, issuing hand-written script amendments each morning prior to shooting. Picking up on the stress that the show's star was under, guest star Mark Eden recalled on *Cult Radio*: "Pat McGoohan was going through a very, very bad time and teetering on the verge of a nervous breakdown because of the pressure on him. I seem to remember that he had a big row with the director, fired him, and directed the rest of the episode himself. It didn't make for a happy time." With his premature departure from the series, Asher moved onto *The Gun Runners*, the second episode filmed for *The Champions*.

The next episode into production was *A Change of Mind*, a script by Roger Parkes, who had switched from a career in agriculture to being a *Daily Express* journalist before landing a job at the BBC as a story editor in 1964. Parkes was working on a script written by Turkish actor/writer Moris Farhi in 1966 when Farhi told him that he was hoping to write for *The Prisoner*.

'The new number two ...' Derren Nesbitt and John Sharp step into the role of village supremo.

59

Angela Browne checks her makeup during shooting of the woodland scenes on *A Change of Mind*

Parkes was keen to write a script of his own rather than edit, so Farhi arranged for Markstein to brief him at MGM. Having been influenced by both the 1959 thriller novel *The Manchurian Candidate* by Richard Condon (in which a captured American soldier is brainwashed to assassinate a politician) and the communist 'witch hunts' conducted by Senator Joseph McCarthy in the US in the early 1950s, Parkes also drew upon the effect of drugs and lobotomies as discussed by his psychiatrist brother for a story where Number 6 was tricked into believing that he had undergone a lobotomy.

Shooting began in late January with *Daily Cinema* listing '*Change of Mind* […] directed by Roy Rossotti' on Wednesday 25 January and Wednesday 1 February. Rossotti was a keen, gauche young art director who had handled second unit work for the film *Doctor Zhivago* and then directed an episode of *The Avengers* in October 1966. The first morning's shoot went badly with McGoohan finding it difficult to follow Rossotti's direction. The cast broke for lunch. Talking to Stephen Ricks on *The Prisoner Investigated*, second assistant director John O'Conner recalled that when the unit returned from lunch "Patrick [came] onto the floor [...] saying, 'The director's not very well and he won't be back after lunch. Will you arrange a car for him to be taken back to London?'" This was McGoohan easing the blow that he had fired Rossotti and taken over himself. On the finished episode, McGoohan took the directing credit under the name 'Joseph Serf'. "That was a fictitious name I made up,"

McGoohan told *PrimeTime*, "Somebody, I think Bernie Williams [...] said, 'Hey, are you going to put yourself down here?' and I said 'No', because [Rossotti] did shoot for a day [...]. He said, 'What do we put down?' and I said, 'Well, James [sic], erm ... Serf.' He said, 'OK' and went off [...] It was the first thing that came into my head. There was probably a picture of an ocean or something on my desk at the time."

Elsewhere at MGM, *Battle Beneath the Earth* wrapped in late January and John S Smith was brought in as a fourth editor by Spencer Reeve to handle *It's Your Funeral* along with Ian Rakoff as his assistant; both were soon acquainted with McGoohan's demanding desires to create something different.

At the end of January, ATV announced Lew Grade's latest three-day sales trip to the USA. While CBS had committed to *The Prisoner*, the movie version of *Koroshi* was sold to their rival ABC. *Broadcast* (1 February 1967) reiterated CBS' purchase of *The Prisoner*, indicating that the series would not appear until Fall 1968. Three days later, *Kinematograph Weekly* commented on the £6.5 million which Grade was spending on his five colour series in production: *The Saint, Man in a Suitcase, The Prisoner,* the Supermarionation show *Captain Scarlet and the Mysterons* (filming at Century 21's Slough studios from Monday 2 January) and *The Champions* (soon to start at ABPC Elstree).

By now, animation for the closing credits had been created. The first piece to end each narrative was described in *Arrival*'s script: 'We continue to move up and away until we have an aerial panoramic view of the Village. Two prison gates suddenly clang shut in foreground. In the centre of screen we see a white dot coming at us like a bullet. It is the face of the Prisoner. It stops just behind the bars.' Three versions ultimately appeared; the first print of *Arrival* showed the bars slamming before the face appeared, a later edit of *Arrival* (plus *A. B. and C.* and *Hammer into Anvil*) saw the face almost filling the screen before the bars slammed, while on the remaining episodes the bars appeared as the face zoomed up. Following this came a twelve-stage process by which the penny-farthing was built, after which the canopy and frame faded to leave the small wheel which became the Earth with the stars of space forming the bigger wheel and canopy. This would also form the basis of the bumper sequences around each commercial break, with the bicycle being disassembled before the adverts and reassembled after the commercials, with a signature tune sting and the series' logo.

The uncredited loudspeaker voice in many episodes was that of Fenella Fielding. "I had worked with Patrick McGoohan on *Danger Man* [*An Affair of State* filmed late 1959] and he wanted me for this part because of my voice," she told Ceidiog Hughes

Serf's up ... a change of director for *A Change of Mind*

# the Prisoner

McGoohan with Fenella Fielding in the Danger Man episode *An Affair of State*

Jack Shampan's set design for *A.B. and C.* and, opposite, as realised on screen

in March 2005, "He didn't explain anything really, he just asked me not to be too sexy. I was there for a morning, at the most it took an hour." On *Britain in a Box*, the actress recalled: "When I arrived, he took me to one side and almost gave me a terrible ticking off, telling me what I was *not* to do before I'd done anything. Once he'd said to me what he said, that was it – I never saw him again."

By February, CBS' Michael Dann was keen to see a finished episode. Grade – who had not seen one himself – wanted to oblige. "Can you put one together for me Pat? I've got the top man coming over from CBS," Lew Grade told McGoohan on the phone. Watching over the editors, the executive producer worked flat out to assemble a print of *Arrival*, delivering it to Grade five days later ... an hour before the CBS meeting. Dann was impressed, but still concerned by Number 6 remaining trapped. "[Michael] said to me, 'I really can't understand what it's all about'," said Grade in *Still Dancing*, "So I said, 'Why don't I fix up a meeting with Patrick McGoohan. He'll explain everything to you'." Grade summoned McGoohan down from the set to meet Dann, and after a vodka-fuelled dinner the CBS man expressed his concerns. According to Dann in *Number Six*, the show's star then replied, "Mr Dann, you have outlined a perfectly wonderful show ... I want you to know that I have changed my mind completely. You make an excellent case. I encourage you ... to make the show you're talking about ... I, of course, will make this show exactly as I am writing, directing and producing it. And therefore, we will both be able to do what we want. Have I made myself clear?"

On *The Persuader*, Grade recalled Dann asked him if he had problems with McGoohan. "I said, 'I never have any problems at all with Patrick McGoohan. He's wonderful.' 'Well, how do you do it?' 'Always give in to what he wants'." Dann returned to New York next day to tell his colleagues that Number 6 would not be turned into a regular TV hero at CBS's request; McGoohan was too strong.

The next episode filmed was a second script by Anthony Skene: *Play In Three Acts*. Speaking to Dave Barrie in *In the Village* Issue 28 (Autumn 2000), Skene recalled that "George [Markstein] was in disfavour by [this time] though still working in his office." David Tomblin asked Skene for an economic script using lots of stock shots, but instead Skene walked around MGM to see what backlots were available. He saw some street sets constructed for the films *Return from the Ashes*, *Up Jumped a Swagman* and *The Liquidator* in 1965, and a French château with bridge built for *The Dirty Dozen*. Using this, his new idea placed Number 6 in these imaginary locations when Number 2 had his dreams manipulated.

The original director on *Play In Three Acts* was the highly experienced Michael Truman. Born in February 1916, Truman had worked on movies since the war, first as an editor at Ealing Studios, then as producer on films like *The Titfield Thunderbolt*. He had directed some *Danger Man* shows in 1960, rejoining the series in 1964 for numerous episodes including *Koroshi*. However, before filming started, Truman was taken ill and replaced by Pat Jackson. The *Daily Cinema* did not list any episode of the series in production on Wednesday 8 February, but for the two weeks after that announced 'Current episode [...] is *Play In Three Acts* directed by Pat Jackson'.

While *The Prisoner* continued filming, British viewers were given their first chance to see the final two *Danger Man* episodes when ATV London screened them at 7.25pm on Sundays 19 and 26 February 1967. The following week, the station screened a few *Danger Man* repeats at 6.30pm on Saturdays.

By now, CBS no longer considered *The Prisoner* for the Fall season. *Variety* reported on Wednesday 22 February that the network had committed for 'a cycle' of the series which was 'most likely [to] be put on the shelf and used as a midseason or summer replacement.' In the *Abilene Reporter* (26 February 1967), Clay Gowran spoke to Dann about *The Prisoner* after he 'committed CBS to purchase at least 17 episodes of the series, a multi-million dollar deal, just on the strength of reading one Prisoner script'. Since then, Dann had viewed *Arrival* and was convinced that "this will be the most talked-about series ever when it goes on the air – it's the most amazing thing I've ever seen in 19 years of programming." Hinting that the show concerned a Drake-style character quitting his job and being transported to an island colony, Dann continued: "So help me, I don't know [who is running the colony], and I bought the series. When I met with McGoohan in London, I asked that same question three times, and he wouldn't answer. The viewer's going to have to decide for himself."

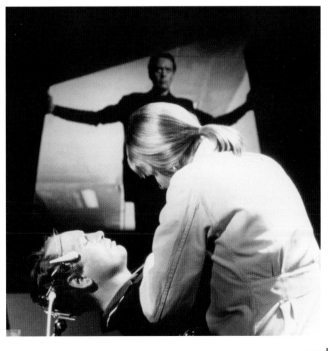

On Monday 27 February, Hammer's *Quatermass and the Pit* started shooting at MGM through to Tuesday 25 April. By late February, rough assemblies of the first seven episodes of *The Prisoner* had been completed. Bob Dearberg left for a new job on *Captain Scarlet and the Mysterons* and was replaced by Eric Mival.

The next episode filmed was *The General*, written by Lewis Greifer as a social comment on the subject of rote learning in education which his sons were experiencing at school, a notion which delighted McGoohan. For his script, Greifer used the pen-name 'Joshua Adam' (the names of his sons) as

Make-up adjustments on *The General*

he had on series episode credits (to differentiate it from his plays) since 1961 on editions of ATV's *Deadline Midnight, 24 Hour Call, Ghost Squad* and *Emergency Ward 10*. The episode was to have been directed by Robert Lynn. Born in Fulham in July 1918, Lynn had directed episodes of film series such as *Dial 999* in the 1950s and had worked on *Ghost Squad* and *The Saint* for ATV. However, Lynn instead went to *Captain Scarlet...* and at a weekend's notice, McGoohan telephoned Peter Graham Scott whom he had worked with on *Danger Man* in 1959/60. Born in 1923, Graham Scott had become an editor in the 1940s and then a director in documentaries, moving into television plays and also film series such as *Zero One* and *The Avengers*, while also working at the BBC as a producer on series like *Mogul* (and its sequel *The Trou-*

*bleshooters*). McGoohan arranged with Sydney Newman, the Head of BBC Television Drama, for Graham Scott to be released from *The Troubleshooters* for a fortnight from Monday 27 February. The *Daily Cinema* listed '*The General* directed by Peter Graham Scott' on both Wednesdays 1 and 8 March, while referring to the episode as *As You Were, General* on Wednesday 15. Colin Gordon – a regular from *The Baron* – remained as Number 2, having played this part in *Play In Three Acts*.

By now, the closing title animation was being revised. At the end, the smaller of the two wheels started spinning to form the Earth while the larger spread out as the universe behind it until a circle reading 'POP' (a word chanted during *Degree Absolute*) zoomed up and filled the screen. Wilf Thompson also revised the Rover sound effect to something close to the half-human noise McGoohan had in mind. This now included elements such as shotgun pellets running around an inflated inner tube and the sound of monks' chant played in reverse, while the roar was the slowed down sound of a man's scream reverberating in a hall at the London School of Physics.

After the previously abandoned theme tunes, the task of scoring of *The Prisoner* was given to a duo from the music company Chappell who had successfully composed both theme and incidentals for *Man in a Suitcase*: Ron Grainer and Albert Elms. Born in Queensland. Australia in 1922, Grainer came to England in 1952 and went on to compose striking television themes such as *Maigret* and *Steptoe and Son*. The main melody for the theme was apparently a tune which McGoohan came up with and passed to Grainer. A demo version of this, entitled *The Age of Elegance*, was recorded by Grainer playing an electronic harpsichord with clavichord, lute and percussion. McGoohan approved, but it was felt that this would need beefing up into something more strident; the star was keen to play percussion himself, having retained the drum kit he played as a jazz drummer in the film *All Night Long* shot in July/August 1961.

Grainer's theme was recorded at Denham from 2pm on Sunday 5 March, performed by two trumpets, two flugelhorns, two bass trumpets, an organ, a piano, two electric guitars (played by Martin Kershaw and Vic Flick), a bass guitar (played by Terry Walsh), an acoustic bass, timpani, drums and percussion. Although the counter-themes and tempo at first caused some confusion, after several takes three versions of the theme (100-second standard opening, 150-second long opening for *Arrival* and 66-second closing version) were recorded. 'I always remember [McGoohan] taking Ron outside and really imploring him to beef it up somewhat, almost ranting and raving,' wrote Eric Mival in his autobiography *Cutting Edge: My Life in Film and Television* (Quoit Media, 2016), 'Ron […] was not best pleased with Pat's insistence to make the whole thing feel more pacey.'

By now the last two scripts for the initial run of thirteen had been selected. Since four more to fulfil CBS' order would be filmed after a summer break, McGoohan did not need to write his concluding episode yet. The first of the concluding pair of episodes was *Hammer into Anvil*, a black comedy of Number 6 taking vengeance on Number 2 for the death of a fellow inmate, written by humourist and poet Roger Woddis. Born in London in May 1917, Woddis' intended career was in medicine, but instead he turned to writing, joining the left-wing Unity Theatre in the 1930s and after the war writing for BBC radio from 1947. A devout communist, he contributed a satirical column for the *Daily Herald* as well as to BBC TV's

Original script for *Hammer into Anvil*

A bicycle made for 2? Patrick Cargill in *Hammer into Anvil*

*That Was The Week That Was*. *The Prisoner* was a rare television drama script for him, although Woddis – like Anthony Skene – had been working on the new ABC series *Haunted*.

The remaining slot was taken by *Many Happy Returns*, Skene's third script. In this, Number 6 woke to find the Village deserted and returned to London for his birthday. The fact that the first act had no dialogue appealed to Tomblin, while Markstein felt this submission was a signpost for the way ahead on the show.

The shooting scripts of *Hammer into Anvil* and *Many Happy Returns* carried a revised variation on the standard 'link sequence' with the new Rover. In this, P asked "Where am I?" over a library shot of the Village, after which there was an optical zoom in on Number 2's Green Dome and a library shot of the black chair rising and turning (from *Arrival*). As the unseen Number 2 spoke from the chair – "In the village" – P was seen running in silhouette on the screen. While P ran along the beach, his voice asked, "What do you want?" A library shot of the 'green eye' in the Control Room backed Number 2's reply: "Information." On Number 2's screen, the silhouette stopped running as P's voice asked, "Whose side are you on?" "That would be telling," replied Number 2, "We want information." The silhouette on the screen shook a fist, saying "You won't get it," and ran away, followed by a silhouetted Rover. As Rover herded P back to the village, Number 2 proclaimed, "By hook or by crook …" after which Number 2's identity was revealed as he/she said, "We will." Silhouetted on the screen, P fell to Rover in combat. As Rover floated away, P rose, asking, "Who are you?" "The new Number 2," replied the voice. "Who is Number 1?" asked P, to be greeted by gentle laughter, as Number 2 replied, "You are our Number 6." "I am not a number. I am a free man," declared P as the image moved in fast on the silhouette of his head, freeze framing as Number 2's echoing, mocking laughter was heard.

While work continued on *The General* at MGM, a second unit helmed by Tomblin returned to Portmeirion for two weeks of shooting from Sunday 5 March. Much of this was inserts with crowd artistes for *Degree Absolute, It's Your Funeral, A Change of Mind, The General* and *Play In Three Acts*, with Frank Maher generally doubling as Number 6. Also scheduled were more extensive Village sequences for *Hammer into Anvil* and *Many Happy Returns*; for these, McGoohan travelled up from London at weekends to work with directors Pat Jackson and Michael Truman. Some of the raft scenes for *Many Happy Returns* were filmed close to St Tudwal's Island near Abersoch. One weekend, McGoohan filmed at MGM until 7.30pm on Friday, drove up to Portmeirion, worked all day Saturday, drove back at 9.30pm to reach his office at 4am and did some paperwork before getting home for breakfast.

Some changes had been made to Portmeirion since September; the piazza pool had been repainted, the Salutation now had a baroque gable and bal-

A university degree in three minutes, maybe, but a whole episode takes somewhat longer. Filming *The General* at MGM

'Pat-a-cake, pat-a-cake...'
Number 2 descends into
paranoia in *Hammer into Anvil*

ustrade, and the portrait of Queen Elizabeth II had vanished from the rear of the Battery Stores (the 1938 garage used as the General Store in the series). Around this time, Clough Williams-Ellis and other local figures were finally able to see *The Prisoner* when Tomblin arranged for *Arrival* to be screened at the Coliseum one Sunday. "When seen in colour at the local cinema," wrote Clough in *Portmeirion: The Place and its Meaning*, "Portmeirion itself seemed to me, at least, to steal the show from its human cast."

Meanwhile, the show's new incidental score was being written by Albert Elms. Born in Milton, Kent in February 1920, Elms served with the Royal Marines in which he was a musician. Elms was a major contributor of incidental music to television film series in the 1950s and 1960s such as *The Adventures of Robin Hood*, as well as movies like *The Breaking Point*. Elms found the series a difficult project to work on as he told David Waters in *Number Six* Issue 2 (Winter 1984/85), "I know that a lot of the crew didn't know what the hell it

'Du musst amboss oder hammer sein.' Filming *Hammer into Anvil.* Patrick Cargill would stay on to portray Thorpe in *Many Happy Returns* (below)

was about – I'm afraid I was one of them." Orchestral scores for *Degree Absolute* and *Play in 3 Acts* [sic] were recorded at Denham on Tuesday 21 March.

On the same day, an ATV press announcement indicated that ITC New York executive Abe Mandell had visited Japan, where he was holding out for the best deals on *The Prisoner* and *Man in a Suitcase*. Back at MGM, *Hammer into Anvil* was directed by Pat Jackson, as noted by the *Daily Cinema* on Wednesdays 22 and 29 March. At the same time, the second unit were still doing inserts for other episodes at MGM; work on Wednesday 22 and 29 March included inserts for *It's Your Funeral*, *Play In Three Acts*, *A Change of Mind*, *The Schizoid Man*, *Hammer into Anvil*, *Free For All* and *The General*.

At the end of March, the film *Dark of the Sun* (shooting in Jamaica since January) arrived at MGM to shoot interiors to mid-May. The first few finished episodes with the Grainer/Elms music were now being completed. The closing animation was changed again, omitting the end of the "POP" version and cutting to footage of Rover at sea from *Free For All*. On the finished shows, this ran to different lengths. Sometimes the animated bicycle was not even completed (*Dance of the Dead*, *The Chimes of Big Ben*, *It's Your Funeral*), sometimes it completed (*The Schizoid Man*, *The General*, *A. B and C.*, *Many Happy Returns*, *Do Not Forsake Me Oh My Darling*, *Living in Harmony*, *The Girl Who Was Death*) and on other occasions it even faded to the two wheels (*Free For All*,

*Checkmate, Once upon a Time, A Change of Mind, Hammer into Anvil*). On *Fall Out*, the bicycle image was completed and held without cutting to Rover.

Production on the first thirteen editions drew to a close in April; by comparison, *Man in a Suitcase* had filmed seventeen episodes by this time and was due to film another thirteen after only a three-week break. Late August was set as the date for work to recommence on *The Prisoner*, but by now it was clear that some of the team would not return. Sidney Palmer departed after a bit of friction, Tony Sloman felt that the series was getting difficult because of McGoohan's overwork, Geoffrey Foot moved on to the movie *Hammerhead* shooting from September, and Bernard Williams went to work on *Battle of Britain* which was being set up for spring 1968. Leaving for *Man in a Suitcase*, Jack Lowin told Steven Ricks in *In the Village* Issue 32 (Summer 1992) that he was relieved to move on: "I'm a great admirer of Pat's – but it was not what one would describe as a 'happy' series to work on."

Michael Truman's poor health meant that he would not complete *Many Happy Returns*. Second unit cameraman Robert Monks told Steven Ricks on *The Prisoner Investigated*, "Michael […] and Pat just didn't see eye to eye. And Michael wasn't in the best of form at the time." Under his 'Joseph Serf' alias, McGoohan again took over as director. Josie Fulford – who had worked on the colour *Danger Man* episodes – took on continuity duties from Doris Martin. Speaking to Sidney Cole for the BECTU History Project (16 August 1988), Doris said of McGoohan by this point: "It was stupid, it was beyond him. He tried to do everything himself and he couldn't."

Featuring Patrick Cargill, who had just guested as Number 2 in *Hammer into Anvil*, *Many Happy Returns* saw additional location filming at Beachy Head near East-

'Anyone at home'? Not quite a 'happy return' for a disillusioned George Markstein

bourne in East Sussex; around Folkestone; at Chalgrove Airfield just south of Oxford; and around London (including Park Lane by Marble Arch, Apsley House, the Wellington Memorial at Duke of Wellington Place, Stag Place and Buckingham Place). On Sunday 16 April, the KAR120C demonstrator Lotus was borrowed again for its final scenes in the series, prior to its sale at the end of the month. Scenes of Number 6 attempting to escape by helicopter were filmed on the MGM lot with the Alouette used at Portmeirion which had been re-registered in February as G-AVEE for UK use by RBA Helicopters of White Waltham Aerodrome near Maidstone, Kent.

*Many Happy Returns* saw George Markstein reprising his title sequence cameo shortly before he left the series. The script editor was badly disillusioned with the use of his writers' ideas and the way that McGoohan was developing the show as an outlandish allegory. Markstein still admired many of McGoohan's qualities such as his intuition, commenting in *Escape*, "He was a superb actor. He had immense ability but he was an egomaniac [...] Some of his writing is as bad as some of my acting would be." The main problem, as he explained when interviewed for *Six into One*, was that "McGoohan was writing, was conceiving, was directing ... and didn't know where he was going. My presence was superfluous."

Had he remained on the series, Markstein would have stuck to his initial vision. "*The Prisoner* was originally planned for 26 episodes with the basic concept developing out into the world," he told Roger Goodman in *Alert* (Summer 1977). In *Escape* he explained that the new episodes would have taken "the Prisoner out of the Village into the world outside [exploring] the whole area of the man finding that he is trapped universally and cannot escape." Number 6 would always be a prisoner of circumstance, even as a free man. With his co-written screenplay for the Oakhurst Films thriller *Robbery* filming since Monday 6 March, Markstein went to Rediffusion to write four episodes of the children's adventure series *Send Foster* which entered production in May for broadcast from July. He also resumed contributions to the *TV Times* from May on subjects such as the NASA space mission, and by the autumn would be the story editor on ABC's *Armchair Theatre*.

On Wednesday 12 April, *Daily Cinema* noted 'Current episode [...] is *Many Happy Returns* directed by Michael Truman [...] Last in the current series. New series begins in August.' *The Prisoner* would continue, but with Patrick McGoohan and David Tomblin now sourcing their own stories.

# 5: "WE HAD TO THINK UP OUTRAGEOUS STORIES"

**J**ust as George Markstein was leaving, assistant film editor Ian Rakoff attempted to pitch a Western idea which Tony Sloman jokingly entitled *Do Not Forsake Me Oh My Darling* in reference to the song from the 1952 Western movie *High Noon*. A similar notion had also been suggested by Frank Maher as he recalled on *Cult Radio*: "We were sitting in the pub after playing squash […] and I said, 'Why don't you make a western?' And [Patrick McGoohan] said, 'What a good idea.'" However, Rakoff's notion was inspired by Issue 70 of Dell's *Gene Autry Comics* from December 1952, and a story in which Autry arrived in a town called Harmony where the sheriff did not permit guns to be worn. With Markstein gone, McGoohan asked Rakoff to develop a script with him … although as time wore on the star became increasingly remote.

Various stories for the series were taken to outline or script level before being abandoned. Inspired by escape committees formed by World War II Prisoners of War, in Autumn 1966 Gerald Kelsey had scripted *Don't Get Yourself Killed* in which Number 6 reluctantly joined an Escape Committee and became caught up in a plan to escape with a stash of gold. From around the same time, Moris Farhi had spent a week drafting *The Outsider* in which Number 6 encountered a pilot who had parachuted clear of a plane crash and planned another escape with him. "[McGoohan] turned it down flat because I had a scene with him perspiring under torture. 'Heroes don't sweat', he said," Farhi recalled to Anthony Masters in the *Telegraph Sunday Magazine* (24 March 1985). A story idea about a computer analyst was offered by John Kruse, who had written extensively on *The Saint*, while Donald Tosh offered Markstein a tale of Number 6 recognising a fellow prisoner as French writer and avia-

'Goodnight children...'
Telling an 'outrageous story'
in *The Girl Who Was Death*

tor Antoine de Saint-Exupéry who went missing in July 1944. David Whitaker had also discussed a story idea for the show, having worked with Markstein in 1966 on two movie scripts called *Time to Run* and *Under-tow*.

The editing team had heard that *The Prisoner* was running low on story ideas, and many of the crew pitched potential outlines to David Tomblin and Patrick McGoohan. Eric Mival offered two ideas: *Ticket to Eternity* in which the Villagers were gripped by a strange religion and Number 2 experimented with time travel; and *Friend or Foe* in which a powerful black orator, Mike X, became a source of intrigue for Number 6. Story ideas were also submitted by film editor John S Smith, sound

# the prisoner

*Ice Station Zebra*, promoted in ABC Cinemas' *Film Review* magazine (December, 1969)

'Three nervous breakdowns' – the pace remains relentless for McGoohan

editor Ken Rolls, assistant director John O'Connor and film librarian Tony Sloman, who wrote an outline with his flatmate, John Whitmarsh-Knight.

Post-production on the episodes continued with Albert Elms' score for *The General* recorded at Denham on Monday 24 April. Another session on Tuesday 9 May then saw the incidentals for *Free For All* and *Hammer into Anvil* recorded, along with specific cues for *It's Your Funeral* and *Arrival*. Three weeks later, Elms was visited by McGoohan, who seemed unhappy that *The Prisoner* was getting out of hand, fearing it would end up like a James Bond movie. Elms agreed to return to score further episodes, passing work on *The Champions* over to Edwin Astley.

Editing on *The Prisoner* continued at MGM during May, while films like *Inspector Clouseau* and *Attack on the Iron Coast* started shooting. During April, John S Smith had taken a look at an abandoned edit of *Dance of the Dead* undertaken by Geoff Foot and started to recut it into a new form.

Meanwhile, McGoohan was in demand for movie projects. He was offered a lead role in the birth-control comedy *Prudence and the Pill* (based on the 1965 novel) which was due to shoot in London from mid-June, but rejected the part as against his principles. McGoohan was then approached by Hollywood director John Sturges who – since September 1965 – had been attempting to shoot a movie version of *Ice Station Zebra*, Alistair MacLean's 1963 thriller novel. There had been considerable script problems and postponements, but McGoohan had been impressed with Sturges' work, and when offered the role of British intelligence agent David Jones, he read the book and agreed to join the cast at MGM Studios in California to film over the summer. His fee from the picture would keep *The Prisoner* afloat and allow the final four episodes to be made to the high standards he demanded. *Variety* announced *Patrick McGoohan joins Ice Station Zebra* on Monday 29 May, the same day that *TV Guide* in New Zealand carried a chat with McGoohan who feared that details of his new series 'may be stolen by another company'; the journalist revealed that 'a character who seems to resemble "John Drake" after he has left the service and gone into retirement [is] held prisoner by [...] former enemies' in a show described as 'sort of *The Fugitive* [...] in reverse.'

Insert shooting for *The Prisoner* continued during June, with location sea shots for *Many Happy Returns* on Wednesday 7 June. On Monday 19 June, alternate shots of the opening titles' filing cabinet were filmed in French, German, Spanish and Italian for overseas prints. All bar four episodes – *Dance of the Dead, It's Your Funeral, A Change of Mind* and *Many Happy Returns* – had now been completed.

"I've worked my way through three nervous breakdowns," McGoohan said to ATV publicist John K Newnham, "First time, the doctor ordered three weeks off. Last time, he suggested three months. There was only one answer, and that was to keep on working. You can't let up when you're in charge.

[…] It's true that I have been unpredictable and impatient. You get that way when you're working at high pressure. […] But I haven't lost a friend in the unit. Although I've probably now lost the lot through saying that!" McGoohan continued to work flat out at MGM until 4pm on the day of his departure for the USA when, after a shower and change of clothes, he was driven to the airport still dictating letters to his assistant Jimmy Millar.

Shaun Usher of the *Daily Sketch* (2 December 1967) noted that 'ATV gambled big money' on *The Prisoner* and received confirmation from McGoohan, as the star boarded an aircraft for Hollywood, that the final episode of the series – which he planned to start writing during the flight – would resolve everything. Shooting on *Ice Station Zebra* commenced on Monday 19 June and scheduled to continue until Thursday 7 September. As such, McGoohan would be in Hollywood when *The Prisoner* resumed filming in late August. Hurriedly, Tomblin came up with a notion to allow another actor to play Number 6 for an episode, giving his idea to Vincent Tilsley to develop under the title *Face Unknown*, with instructions that Village scenes requiring Portmeirion should be minimal. After a story where a conjurer arrived in the Village and made Number 6 vanish in a magic cabinet was rejected, Tilsley desperately offered the notion of Number 6's mind being placed in another man's body. Tomblin also revived an unused outline he had developed of a spoof episode for *Danger Man*, giving it to Terence Feely to write as *The Girl Who Was Death*. When this script was accepted, an attempt was made to expand it into a two-part story (for potential use as a feature like *Koroshi*), but this was quickly squashed by Lew Grade.

Face unknown: with McGoohan in Hollywood, Nigel Stock takes the starring role in *Do Not Forsake Me Oh My Darling*

Rakoff's Western, now known as *Living in Harmony*, would complete scripting in collaboration with Tomblin during McGoohan's absence. This working partnership was not good, and after several meetings Tomblin announced that Rakoff had contributed as much as possible, so he would now take over writing, paying Rakoff his full fee and commenting "Count yourself lucky that you'll be out of this mess."

The three new stories largely abandoned McGoohan's format, and he referred to them as "padding" when speaking in 1979. "We had to think up outrageous stories outside the theme" he explained, "We tried to have fun with them and make them as visually exciting as possible." Tomblin was also aware that Everyman's method of working was not quick enough for ATV, telling Steven Ricks on *The Prisoner Investigated*, "We tried to make them so well – like feature films […] If we'd carried on, we wouldn't have met the showing dates."

As the first thirteen episodes were completed during July, editors were laid off with a fortnight's notice, and John S Smith moved on to edit

'Do we know where Seltzman is?'
Nigel Stock, Zena Walker and
Clifford Evans in *Do Not Forsake
Me Oh My Darling*

*Submarine X-1*, which started shooting at MGM from Sunday 16 July. Some of the episodes had now been retitled: *The Queen's Pawn* was *Checkmate*, *Degree Absolute* became *Once upon a Time* and *Play In Three Acts* was rechristened *1, 2 and 3* then *A. B. and C*. ATV Information began releasing promotional material: 'Who is The Prisoner? Where is the strange Village which is his prison? Why is he there? … These are just a few of the questions viewers will be asking when ATV's newest hour-long thriller film series begins in the autumn.'

On Monday 24 July, *Variety* announced that John Sturges would have problems completing *Ice Station Zebra* to schedule, in order to allow McGoohan to return to the UK for *The Prisoner*. A syndicated piece by Ivor Davis (originally dated Thursday 27 July) appeared in various US papers such as the *Kingston Gleaner* from Friday 4 August. Under the title *'Danger Man's new number'*, the journalist pondered that McGoohan's new series 'may be a tremendous flop. Not because [it] is unimaginative or too ordinary but [because it] may be too original.' The article explained that the star had been putting in sixteen-hour days on *The Prisoner* ('a shocking and refreshingly new type of 60-minute thriller') of which the journalist had seen one episode, describing it as 'one of the most unusual serials ever made for television' and 'a kind of modern-day science-fiction story.' Davis felt that the show would have either 'an enormous impact on the TV-watching public or fall flat on its face [because] it is a thinking man's show' and might be 'too sophisticated.' The *Washington Post* carried comments from McGoohan on Friday 4 August in Dorothy Manners' piece *'Secret Agent' Star Quitting TV Cold*; this saw the actor condemn television's appetite for product, noting that he had turned down CBS's request to film 36 segments of *The Prisoner*. "I have completed 13 and will do four more – and then no more," declared the actor.

Emphasising *The Prisoner*, ATV announced their autumn line-up. *Television Today* (10 August 1967) confirmed that *The Prisoner* would run for thirteen weeks at 7.25pm on Sundays from 1 October to 31 December; this applied to ATV London which would debut *Captain Scarlet and the Mysterons* the same day and *Man in a Suitcase* a day earlier. In the *Daily Telegraph* (11 August 1967), Peter Knight reported that 'ATV are reluctant to reveal the format […] apart from saying that it is a complete breakaway from the present spy fiction trend.' In *Kinematograph Weekly* (19 August 1967), Tony Gruner noted that ATV's new season had five colour series (which UK viewers could only see in monochrome), emphasising that *The Prisoner* ('created by McGoohan in association with George Markstein') had already been snapped up by CBS.

Tomblin performed rewrites on *Face Unknown* in mid-August, while filming on *The Prisoner* resumed on Saturday 26 with Nigel Stock taking centre stage in *Face Unknown* as the Colonel whose body contained Number 6's mind. Pat Jackson returned as director. Ronald Liles of Ardmore Studios took over as production manager on the series, having handled some of the later work on *2001: A Space Odyssey*. Len Harris, who had worked at Gainsborough Pictures and Hammer, became the main camera operator, having briefly worked on the 1966 Portmeirion shoot. From Century 21, John Lageu joined the team, and soon replaced incoming set dresser Colin Southcott, while David Naughton was the new film librarian. Frank Turner, Olive Mills and Dora Lloyd were now on make-up, hairdressing and wardrobe respectively, while Ann Besserman took over continuity.

A minimal crew made a final visit to Portmeirion to shoot location inserts for *Face Unknown* with Maher as Number 6. Location filming also included London venues such as Buckingham Place and the Victoria Colonnade on Southampton Row, and closer to the studios at GEC-Marconi on Elstree Way, the A1081 London Colney bypass and Elstree's A41 roundabout. Since KAR120C had been sold and Lotus were no longer involved with the Super Seven, Everyman contacted Peter Warr of the Barnet Motor Company who located a similar model, LCK88D, which had just been sold to his friend Frank Rycroft; this was loaned and fitted with fake number plates.

By late August, ATV Midlands schedulers were aware that ITV's run of *The Prisoner* would comprise seventeen episodes since *Arrival* was referred to as 1/1/17 (i.e. Series 1, Episode 1 of 17); by contrast Scottish TV's schedules had the annotation 1/1/13, suggesting only thirteen episodes. ITC's brochure to market *The Prisoner* worldwide presented images of Portmeirion and the blazered McGoohan, selling the show as 'the most challenging and unusual series ever filmed for television [...] It is a series with depth: stories that will make viewers think and, at the same time, will keep them on the edge of their seats with excitement as the Prisoner resists every mental and physical effort to break him.'

Mike Tomkies of the *Daily Mail* interviewed McGoohan under the title *I live as if I was waiting for a bullet to hit me* (1 September 1967). Speaking in the US, the star explained: "*The Prisoner* is all about freedom. It's about a top scientist who has vital space secrets in his head and decides he wants to resign [...] I *hope* it's exciting entertainment. It's a way-out series of course."

In fact, Canada was the first country to screen *The Prisoner* via CTV

## I live as if I was waiting for a bullet to hit me

### DANGER MAN TALKING

HOLLYWOOD, Thursday

ROCK HUDSON stood on one side of him, Ernest Borgnine on the other. A formidable combination, perhaps, but Patrick McGoohan, making his Hollywood debut in M.G.M.'s £3,000,000 film, Ice Station Zebra, seemed not one jot overawed.

In fact, he was up to all his old tricks—behaving with that

### by MIKE TOMKIES

*Daily Mail* (1 September 1967)

*Do Not Forsake Me Oh My Darling:* Jack Shampan visualises the mind swap control room

# the prisoner

On air in Canada: *The Telegram*, (6–13 October 1967)

'How about the old bicycle?' McGoohan in Astrakhan hat and Kosho gear at the *Prisoner* press conference

channels such as CFTO (Channel 9 in Toronto) and CKCO (Channel 13 in Kitchener). *Arrival* made its worldwide broadcast debut on Tuesday 5 September, after which the stations aired *A. B. and C*, *Free For All*, *The Schizoid Man*, *The General*, *Hammer into Anvil*, *It's Your Funeral*, *Many Happy Returns*, *A Change of Mind*, *Checkmate*, *Dance of the Dead*, *Once upon a Time* and *The Chimes of Big Ben* through to Tuesday 28 November before replacing the series with *The Avengers*.

The Evelyn Waugh adaptation *Decline and Fall* (latterly *Decline and Fall of a Birdwatcher*) started a three-month shoot at MGM on Monday 4 September, alongside *Face Unknown*, which was completed upon McGoohan's return from Hollywood midway through the month. Joining the team as editor for this episode was Eric Boyd-Perkins who had worked on various Hammer movies.

Ron Grainer's theme tune was re-recorded commercially by RCA from 10am on Friday 15 September at Regent Sound on Tottenham Court Road, London. "I was very sorry that when [Ron] brought it out on record that he reverted to his *original* way of doing it which was very bland indeed," commented Eric Mival in *Village World* (Number Six, 1987).

With McGoohan temporarily back from Hollywood pending further work on *Ice Station Zebra*, *Living in Harmony* went before the cameras in mid-September with Tomblin on his first solo directing assignment. Phyllis Townshend joined the team to handle continuity, having been contracted by Tomblin as she finished another film at MGM; also on board was sound recordist Cyril Swern who had worked on *Danger Man* from September to December 1964. The episode made heavy use of the backlot previously seen as the Village, but also indulged a day's location shooting at Five Knolls on Dunstable Downs.

Joining the cast for *Living in Harmony* was French-born Canadian actor Alexis Kanner whom Tomblin had befriended in May 1962 on the film *We Joined The Navy*. Born in May 1942, Kanner had appeared on stage with the RSC (including Peter Brook's *Theatre of Cruelty* project) and had featured as Detective Constable Matt Stone on BBC1's police series *Softly, Softly* in early 1966 since when he had made the independent film *The Ernie Game* in Montreal during January/February 1967 and in late June had recorded *Cinéma Vérité* for *Love Story*. In Six of One's *Under the Spotlight*, Kanner recalled opposition to his casting: "Rose Tobias Shaw […] said 'You can't have him. You can't use him.' And Patrick said, 'Why not?' And she said, 'He'll tear up the scenery!'"

During filming on *Living in Harmony*, the series' press launch was staged at MGM on Wednesday 20 September. Journalists were first shown two episodes on a big screen and then led through to a sound stage where, to one side, was the caged room seen in *Once upon a Time*, inside which was McGoohan wearing a Astrakhan hat and a long crimson Kosho tunic from *It's*

*Your Funeral*. The star and two waiters in Village garb offered drinks through the bars. Also present was Angelo Muscat. Ignoring questions, McGoohan instead asked the reporters for their impressions of his show. "What about that big ball?' What do you think it was supposed to be made of? What did it represent? Did it represent anything to you? What significance did it have? ... How about the old bicycle? Do you think that has any special significance? Did you think there was a science-fiction element in the story?" recalled journalist Anthony Davis in the Southern *TV Times* (14-20 October 1967). The actor posed for photographs with the penny-farthing and a Moke, after which a curtain was drawn back to reveal the Number 2 chair, around which was a buffet and two waitresses beneath design paintings by Jack Shampan. McGoohan departed and returned in a normal suit to watch Alexis Kanner clown around on the penny-farthing, after which he donned his Western garb for *Living in Harmony* and made his goodbyes. "No actor has ever been more closely identified with a series," commented an ATV official of McGoohan to the *Daily Mirror* (21 September 1967).

To balance out accessible plots and Portmeirion-heavy episodes, the initial UK running order was decided upon as *Arrival, The Chimes of Big Ben, A. B. and C., Free For All, The Schizoid Man, The General, Many Happy Returns, Dance of the Dead, Face Unknown, It's Your Funeral, Checkmate, Living in Harmony, A Change of Mind, Hammer into Anvil, The Girl Who Was Death, Once upon a Time* and finally the yet-to-be-filmed conclusion. Previewing the autumn line-up on Sunday 24 September, the *Observer* referred to *The Prisoner* as 'Tele-Kafka'. Three ITC series were set to debut at the end of September. In the Midlands weekday franchise, ATV launched *Man in a Suitcase* at 8pm on Wednesday 27, with *Captain Scarlet and the Mysterons* at 5.25pm on Friday 29 followed at 7.30pm by *The Prisoner*. *The Prisoner* took over its slot from re-runs of *The Saint*, and *Danger Man* had concluded its long repeat run in the 10.30pm slot the previous Friday. The week *The Prisoner* debuted, BBC1's opposition was the popular Hippodrome Circus from Great Yarmouth whereafter the popular imported American film series *Daktari* about an African wildlife reserve ran against Number 6 on Fridays.

'Tele-Kafka' – and *The Observer* hasn't even seen *Fall Out* yet

*TV World*, the Midlands' listing magazine, gave substantial coverage to the ITC offerings on its cover, proclaiming *New Autumn Shows* (23-29 September 1967). Inside, a feature entitled *Action this Autumn!* carried a shot of McGoohan from *Free For All* with an introduction about the Village: 'All exits are cut off by a deadly ray barrier [...] All the villagers have been concerned with national secrets in the outside world and have been brought to the village, where their secrets can be safely pressed by an unknown power.'

*Television Today* (28 September 1967) oddly chose a shot of a moustachioed Number 6 from *The Schizoid Man* to promote the series. Running a week behind the Midlands, in London the *TV Times* (30 September – 6 October 1967) promoted *The Prisoner* with Russell Allison's item *New for London*. Amidst four colour shots, the article explained: 'There has never been a better kept secret than this one. The studio sound stages have been barred since the day filming began. For McGoohan believes that he is breaking into completely new television territory – in presentation and stories alike […] He has taken over direction of many of the sequences (but without giving himself a screen credit for this) […] And he has worked on every script, irrespective of who may have written it. "So," he says, "if people don't like it, there's only one person to blame – me!".' McGoohan found 'a village somewhere in Britain in which to film […] but is refusing to reveal where it is. It's part of the mystery.' The star emphasised: "There is no connection with *Danger Man*: you are not going to see a follow-up to that series." Meanwhile, *TV World* (30 September – 6 October 1967) was promoting *The Chimes of Big Ben* before *Arrival* had even aired and ran an interview with 39 year-old bachelor Angelo Muscat who commented, "My part is such a mystery. I don't even know yet whether I'm a goodie or a baddie." The episode billing itself was promoted by a monochrome shot of Number 6's cohort, Nadia.

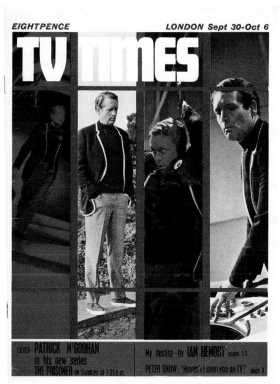

ATV's internal programme schedule for 29 September 1967

*TVTimes* (September 30 – October 6 1967)

    *The Prisoner* debuted on British television at 7.30pm on Friday 29, with the weekly ATV Midlands transmissions from 35mm film prints relayed to viewers tuned to Grampian in Scotland. The broadcast attracted two million viewers, and was generally to have a rating of marginally less than this for the rest of the run.

    Much of the country took *The Prisoner* at 7.25pm on Sundays from ATV London, a slot previously occupied by feature films; this included Southern, Westward (relaying to Channel) and Tyne-Tees. In this slot, BBC1 was repeating the popular sitcom *Steptoe and Son*. An initial 4.8 million viewers caught *Arrival* that Sunday. Television Audience Measurement (TAM) figures for the week showed *The Prisoner* had performed reasonably, ranking seventh in London (with a score of 47) and equal tenth with Tyne Tees (48), although behind *Man in a Suitcase*.

    The first reviews appeared. Looking at ATV's line-up in the *Daily Mail* (2 October 1967), Peter Black observed that *The Prisoner* was 'the most interesting of the bunch […] The appeal lies in figuring up what the hell is going on and whether Drake, or No 6, as he must now be called, will escape.' The critic listed the 'superficial influence' on the series of the James Bond films, *Thunderbirds*, petrol commercials and Jonathan Miller's television film *Alice in Wonderland*, shown in December 1966. Black felt that McGoohan strove

'Well, stranger. Fancy living in Harmony?' Patrick McGoohan films on the MGM backlot

for 'the atmosphere of older fairy tales'. In the *Daily Express* (2 October 1967), James Thomas penned *Prisoner gets away from old routine*, describing the show as 'a strange, original-looking cliffhanger: a real weirdie' and thus 'a bit of a gamble' for a peak spot. 'I imagine its stories will not lift us far out of the TV adventure norm,' he wrote, adding 'the whole atmosphere of the production is bizarre and way out of the ordinary.'

Peter Knight of the *Daily Telegraph* (3 October 1967) called the show 'a tense, teasing drama with a difference'. Noting that he might detect a 'social comment on the freedom of the individual being submerged and smothered by organisation', Knight felt that it was 'certainly no ordinary run-of-the-mill pulp thriller but a stylish, sophisticated, polished production.' 'Patrick McGoohan in Toyland,' was the view of Ann Purser in *Television Today* (5 October 1967). Her review noted that the 'balloon' was 'a really splendid sinister idea'. However, the 'headquarters' were 'too gimmicky, too near to *Captain Scar-*

*let* to sustain the suspense' although *Arrival* was 'fast-moving, smooth and sophisticated in the McGoohan manner.' At 7.30pm on Thursday 5 October, *The Prisoner* made its debut on Scottish Television; just under a million viewers tuned in for *Arrival*, after which the ratings were generally around half a million. Ulster had originally planned to take these transmissions in Northern Ireland, but late in the day decided to defer the series until 1968.

Meanwhile, production on *Living in Harmony* concluded and Mc-Goohan returned to Hollywood for extra filming on *Ice Station Zebra*, as reported by Ronald Simpson of *New Zealand TV Weekly* (9 October 1967). McGoohan's aim was to write a concluding *Prisoner* script during this time, but Sturges' schedule was demanding. When Tomblin took time out from directing *The Girl Who Was Death* to fly out and collect the script, he returned empty-handed. *The Prisoner* was a rarity in television film series in that it would offer a conclusion; in America, *The Fugitive* had just achieved this on Tuesday 29 August 1967 with a two-part wrap-up (filmed in March) which attracted record-breaking audiences for ABC, a success repeated on ITV the next day. Talking to Anthony Masters in the *Sunday Telegraph* (24 March 1985), ITC executive Bernard Kingham recalled, "Lew Grade gave McGoohan carte blanche, but drew a breath of relief when the series was finished."

In the UK, location work for *The Girl Who Was Death* included second unit material at Eltisley Cricket Ground near St Neots as reported in the *St Neots Advertiser* on Tuesday 3 October; in this article, McGoohan's assistant Jimmy Millar commented of the new series (yet to be seen by Anglia viewers) that 'Danger Man resigns and is abducted.' From Monday 9 to Thursday 12, various sequences were filmed without McGoohan at the Kursaal Fun Fair at Southend-on-Sea, Essex and saw a cameo from Alexis Kanner; shooting was covered in the *Southend Standard* on Thursday 12.

'My name ... is Death'
Justine Lord on location
in Southend-on-Sea

To promote *A. B and C.* in *TV World* (7-13 October 1967), a light piece on maid actress Bettine Le Beau and her fascination with pop art appeared in the *People* section. ITC generated numerous 'people' orientated stories for syndication. One was entitled *McGoohan Invites You 'Come Into My Kitchen'* in which 'the feminine viewer' was told about Number 6's 'functional, comfortable and extremely modern' room with 'spacious working spaces [...] a wide counter running [and] a special place is reserved for tall copper canisters containing tea, coffee and sugar [...] Just the sort of kitchen, in fact, that any woman would love to work in!'

On Friday 6 October, Anglia started *The Prisoner* at 8pm on Fridays, a week behind ATV Midlands. In *Kinematograph Weekly* (7 October 1967), Tony Gruner discussed ATV's

Above: 'Ingenious and witty.'
(*The Chimes of Big Ben*)
Below: Ron Grainer's
theme is revisited for single
release. Opposite: sheet music

strong weekend line up, citing Sunday as 'ITV's greatest onslaught' and noting that *The Prisoner* 'with its mysterious overtones and technical wizardry, should secure the highest ratings.' Maurice Wiggin's verdict in the *Sunday Times* on 8 October was that *The Prisoner* was 'ambitious' and judging by *Arrival* it would 'provide fresh and fetching entertainment with that desirable spirit-level quality – well managed, sophisticated physical action, beautifully photographed, plus an unobtrusive suggestion of philosophical depth.' The only problem Wiggin saw was that the 'glittering superstructure of production is not supported by a really adequate story-line.' In the *Sunday Telegraph*, Philip Purser – noting the production company's name suggested an allegory – narrowed the series' locale down to 'Butlin's, Port Meirion … or a country of the mad'. Overlapping the second half of Sunday night screenings from Sunday 8 was *Ironside*, a new imported American detective series retitled *A Man Called Ironside* by the BBC against which *The Prisoner* would fair pretty well.

TAM ratings for the second week were down; *The Prisoner* only charted in Tyne-Tees at equal tenth (51). In the *Daily Mail* (9 October 1967), Peter Black declared, '*The Prisoner* is worth keeping an eye open for [being] stylish and elegant.' The absence of the usual straight-forward narrative 'that moves from start to finish like a fist to the jaw makes it challenging stuff in terms of TV action.' Clifford Davis of the *Daily Mirror* (9 October 1967) felt that the second episode was 'even more intriguing than the first' and declared that 'Patrick McGoohan […] can take a bow here. I'm hooked.'

*Variety* covered *Arrival*'s London debut with Otta's review (11 October 1967) saying it 'deserves full marks for boldness and daring in trying to break out of the formulas of packaged thick-ear stuff.' The format was 'intriguing to the mind' as 'a comment on modern living' but Otta was concerned that 'The content of the first story was thin, but excusable because of its introductory nature […] It's the novelty of the idea that is the main attraction and it remains to see how it grows.'

Promoting *A. B. and C.*, Anthony Davis described the press launch and *The Extraordinary Mr McGoohan* in the Southern edition of the *TV Times* (14-20 October 1967). Discussing McGoohan, Davis noted that at MGM, 'some like him greatly, some are wary of him; all respect him. But then seldom has any actor staked so much on a series. If the series is a hit, the credit will be chiefly his. If audiences find it too bizarre (and I am assured that it becomes more bizarre as it progresses) then he will have to shoulder the blame. The final script has yet to be written. And he has alternative endings in mind.' In *TV World* (14-20 October 1967), *Free For All* was promoted with a *People* piece about guest star Rachel Herbert, while the listing was highlighted in a boxed item offering a photograph of the bloodied Number 6 from the episode's climax.

On Friday 13 October, RCA issued the theme single as *The Prisoner* by The Ron Grainer Orchestra (RCA 1635) backed with *Happening Sunday*.

The theme tune was also available as sheet music from New World Music with a cover showing the boat escape from *Free For All* and a close-up of Number 6; New World also included it alongside the themes for *Captain Scarlet and the Mysterons* and *Man in a Suitcase* in the volume *TV For Brass*.

By mid-October, McGoohan was back at MGM for work on *The Girl Who Was Death*, and had started writing the final episode, *Fall Out*, on the flight back from Hollywood. However, this was apparently unusable. In *Six into One*, Grade recalled McGoohan saying: "'Lew, I just cannot find an ending. I've got too confused with the project.' And I thought that was very nice of him to come straight out with me and admit it. And I told the networks, 'We have no ending'." The unflappable Grade bestowed wisdom to his exhausted star. "I told him to leave it loose," he said to Anthony Masters in the *Telegraph Sunday Magazine* (24 March 1985), "We thought it would cause a reaction but were amazed at how huge that reaction was."

"I envisaged it from the beginning," McGoohan told Anthony Davis of the final instalment in the *TV Times* (17-23 February 1968), "In a series like this, you have to know at the outset what you're aiming at [...] So I had the idea for the final episode first of all and took it from there." Talking to Roger Goodman in 1979, McGoohan elaborated that he had a basic idea only of how the conclusion should play out and the messages it should contain: "But I didn't have that last script in the beginning. In fact, that last script was written by me very close to the end, in 36 hours, just scribbling away and chiselling at it, until eventually I got what we have, which, as far as I am concerned, I think, works. I wouldn't change it."

Philip Purser returned to *The Prisoner* in the *Sunday Telegraph* (15 October 1967) admitting, 'I was perhaps too dismissive last week [...] I think I

'Lew, I just cannot find an ending.' McGoohan prepares to shoot his way out of *Fall Out*

'Bachelor girl' Jane Merrow in *The Schizoid Man*

must have been disappointed by the mixture of styles. I very much like the idea of the little rococo village [but] I am bored by the futuristic Captain Scarlet stuff.' *The Chimes of Big Ben* drew praise for its 'ingenious and witty script' although McGoohan's Number 6 had 'an intensity that I find a bit tiring' with the star hanging his reputation 'on his efforts to prove that you don't always need to aim at the lowest common denominator; I think he's made his point.'

In the north, Border selected the same slot as Scottish, kicking off with *Arrival* at 7.30pm on Thursday 18 October. However, a black-out hit Scottish that night, meaning *A. B. and C.* did not go out, with the station continuing with *Free For All* the following week.

To promote the fourth episode in London, *TV Times* (21-27 October) presented a quartet of vivid colour images of McGoohan from *Free For All* and *Dance of the Dead* on its cover and emphasised *Free For All* in the listings with a shot of Number 2. Promoting *The Schizoid Man*, guest star and 'bachelor girl' Jane Merrow was the subject of an article in the *Women* section of *TV World* (21-27 October 1967).

On Saturday 21 October, *Kinematograph Weekly*'s Tony Gruner noted that the BBC feared positive public reaction to *The Prisoner* in their scheduling of *Ironside*. 'My own feeling is that McGoohan is likely to grow from strength to strength because of [the show's] sheer single-mindedness and technical know-how,' declared Gruner of the "in" series.'

*A. B. and C.* failed to dent the ratings, yet McGoohan did feature in that week's TAM charts for an episode of *Danger Man* shown by Granada. With four episodes of *Danger Man* left to screen by September, Granada was one of the last regions to take *The Prisoner*; *Arrival* did not air until 8pm on Friday 27 October. This netted three and a half million viewers, who generally stuck with the series over the first five weeks. Granada's debut was eighth in the TAM charts (47) and the following week, *The Chimes of Big Ben* maintained this position (48).

'Bloody rubbish'. Don Chaffey on location for *Arrival*

While the critics were impressed, a confused public had been expecting something akin to *Danger Man*. Don Chaffey got first-hand reaction to the shows he directed a year earlier. "I used to go down to my local deliberately on a Sunday night," he recalled on *Six into One*, "I could hear the final bits of *The Prisoner* going on and the landlord would be sitting watching it [saying] 'Pour yourself a beer. I'm watching this bloody rubbish you've been making!' Twenty minutes later there'd be the most almighty row going on with everybody yelling at me, saying what a lot of rubbish it was. I'd ask why they bothered watching it. Despite the arguments they went back for more the following week."

Albert Elms' final music recordings on Monday 23 October covered scores for *Face Unknown* and *Living in Harmony*, plus the spiritual *Dry Bones* for *Fall Out*. At MGM, work continued on *The Girl Who Was Death* through to Thursday 2 November. Location work on the episode near the studio had included material on Shenley Road in Borehamwood; at the Thatched Barn hotel close to the A1; on the A6T at Shenley; the junction of Blanche Lane and St Albans Road in South Mimms;

McGoohan contemplates the end (*Fall Out*)

Well End Lane; the Mops and Brooms pub, Rowley Lane; Buckettsland Lane and the junction of Harris Lane, Mimms Lane and Rectory Lane. Shooting on the lot featured the use of another helicopter, an American Bell 47 D-1, re-registered as G-ATSH in March 1966 and based at Rush Green Aerodrome.

The London *TV Times* (28 October–3 November 1967) confirmed the Village's location in Innes Gray's two-page spread *The Prisoner's Secret Revealed*. Alongside shots of Portmeirion filming and quotes from hotel manager Trevor Williams and Clough Williams-Ellis' secretary Mary Roberts, the journalist commented: 'Shoals of letters have arrived at *TV Times*. All guessed the location correctly.' The same week, the listings magazine *Look Westward* carried a one-page profile of McGoohan entitled *I'm No Prisoner*. To publicise *The General*, *TV World* (28 October – 3 November 1967) ran a piece about how guest star Betty McDowall enjoyed tennis in the *Women* section while the listing was accompanied by a shot of the Professor.

In *Kinematograph Weekly* (28 October 1967), Tony Gruner's championing continued: '*The Prisoner* may not be everyone's cup of tea but the speed of production and the intensity of McGoohan's performance puts this one-hour series in a British class of its own.' On Tuesday 31 October, ATV's latest press bulletin fuelled a story in *Variety* the next day on how Grade was 'glowing over the worldwide success of his new sci-fi-spy series *The Prisoner* [which has] found buyers in all major markets, including the US, Canada, Latin America, Australia, Germany […] and finally Japan.' Grade was 'bullish' over the series'

'You're to go to the Magnum Record Shop.' McGoohan revives his *Danger Man* garb for *The Girl Who Was Death*

impact, feeling it demonstrated how ATV was ahead of the US 'in tv production techniques and ideas.' An impressed CBS was interested in three feature films to be made by McGoohan; one film starring the actor and two others as potential pilots. '*The Prisoner* has turned out to be a gamble which financially has just about paid […] In spite of a production budget in excess of $140,000 per seg, show has regularly been over-budget and developed into the most costly series ever mounted […] However, Grade […] is well satisfied with the prestige of overseas sales.' The story was also covered by Gruner in *Kinematograph Weekly* (4 November 1967). Of the CBS projects, the film was apparently *Brand* to be made in Norway, while another was the *Vagabond* pilot, now entitled *The Outsider*.

Novelist Anthony Burgess, then reviewing television in *The Listener* (2 November 1967), described *The Prisoner* as 'a series on which I'm thoroughly hooked […] The familiar py-thriller […] of the opposed powers has been dropped; the thesis is the contrast between the individual mind that must hold onto its privacy and the nameless collective organisation that will do anything to break that privacy down.' However, he feared 'the display of technical resources is disproportionate to the end they serve. I would go further and say that the end doesn't matter.'

With limited facilities and time, shooting began on *Fall Out* on Thursday 2 November under McGoohan's direction. The actor was aware that already previously loyal fans of *Danger Man* were being thrown off-balance by his new show. 'People expected the same straightforward plots [...] They were disappointed,' he wrote in the foreword for *Cult TV: The Essential Critical Guide by Jon E Lewis and Penny Stempel* (Pavilion Books, 1993).

Redressed sets from *The Girl Who Was Death* formed the backdrops for much of *Fall Out*, and Welsh actor Kenneth Griffith – who had been the guest star in the previous episode – found himself given a new role in the series finale, with Alexis Kanner again a willing participant. After working on *Decline and Fall* on the adjacent sound stage, Leo McKern returned as Number 2, now looking very different; the beard which he had sported in his last two episodes, grown because of his appearance in *Volpone, or The Fox* at the Oxford Playhouse from September 1966 and the Garrick from January 1967, had vanished in favour of the close-cropped look for the movie. Also back was Angelo Muscat, while since filming *Hammer into Anvil* Peter Swanwick had worked on two BBC1 shows, the *Proof Positive* edition of *Softly Softly* and an episode of *Vendetta*, *The Suicide Man*, recorded in mid-April.

*The Day Sinden was Seasick in a Cinema* was the title of a *TV World* article promoting *Many Happy Returns* in its *Series and Serials* section (4-10 November 1967) as guest star Donald Sinden recalled making the film *The Cruel Sea* in 1952, while fellow guest star Georgina Cookson gave her views on family fashion in the pages for *Women*; the programme listing was accompanied by a shot of Number 6 and Sinden's Colonel. In London, J Lennon of

Finchley wrote to the *Viewerpoint* section of the *TV Times* (4-10 November 1967) asking 'I am curious to know why a Penny-Farthing (with a candy-striped shade on top) is shown before and after your weekly series *The Prisoner*.' Beneath a shot of a Kosho-ready McGoohan with the cycle at the press launch, the response from 'a programme company spokesman' was 'This is a symbolic device and the reason for it will be revealed later in the series.'

Lois Dickert Armstrong's interview with McGoohan appeared in the *Los Angeles Times* on Sunday 5 November under the title *Actor McGoohan Sees Films, TV as Blessing and Threat*. Reiterating concerns about invasion of privacy and McGoohan's "moral obligation" to entertain, the setting of *The Prisoner* was described as 'a closed village for retired or incapacitated nuclear scientists.' McGoohan said the Village was not science-fiction, but a contemporary "reflection of the pressure on all of us today to be numbered, to give up our individualism." Planning to film *Brand*, he was abandoning television which would "eventually gobble you up and destroy you."

Amidst work at MGM for *Fall Out*, McGoohan worked on second unit pick-ups for *The Girl Who Was Death* on Shenley Road on Wednesday

'London will lie in ruins!' Kenneth Griffith as Schnipps in *The Girl Who Was Death*

Above: Home at last? Reunited with the Lotus in *Fall Out*.
Opposite: 'Thanks for the trip, dad!' Alexis Kanner

8, but the cavern set on Stage 6 was the main focus for the first few days. That week in the *Your View* section of *TV World* (11-17 November 1967) I Bell of Stoke-on-Trent asked: 'What make of car is it that Patrick McGoohan drives in *The Prisoner*?' 'The car is a yellow and green Lotus made especially for the series,' replied the postbag editor. The same issue offered an article about guest star Mary Morris under the title *Mary's ideal home began life as a cowshed* in the *Series and Serials* section of *TV World* (11-17 November 1967), while the listing for *Dance of the Dead* was promoted with a photograph of various costumed characters. That weekend, Sunday audiences for *The Prisoner* peaked at 5.4 million for *Many Happy Returns*.

Shooting on *Fall Out* continued for another week at MGM while second unit material for *The Girl Who Was Death* was filmed at the Beachy Head lighthouse on Thursday 16. Editing work on *Face Unknown* (or *Faith Unknown* according to some ITV schedules) over-ran. It was originally scheduled to air on ATV Midlands and Grampian on Friday 24 November under its new title, *Do Not Forsake Me Oh My Darling*. However, after *TV World* had gone to print it was decided that *Checkmate* would screen instead. In London, *TV Times* (18-24 November 1967) readers seemed dissatisfied as Miss AP Record of Woking wrote in *Viewerpoint*: 'The most disappointing and ridiculous [series is] *The Prisoner* with Patrick McGoohan.'

Unfortunately, the series' momentum was about to suffer a blow. *The Prisoner* was off the air for ATV London and its affiliates on Sunday 19 November, pre-empted by a networking of *The Royal Variety Performance*. The same day, McGoohan and his team undertook a second unit location shoot for *Fall Out* in London, visiting the Victoria Embankment, Westminster Bridge, the House of Lords and Buckingham Place; a third Lotus was used on the series, sporting fake plates as KAR 120C and driven by Graham Nearn of Caterham. The following week it was back to the soundstages at MGM for more interiors.

To make up for the earlier black-out, Scottish deferred broadcast of *Dance of the Dead* from Thursday 23 and instead screened *A. B. and C.. The Prisoner* graced a colour inner page in *TV World* (25 November – 1 December 1967) with a bright shot from *It's Your Funeral*, accompanied by a note explaining that this episode would in fact air *next* week; the same issue carried Mike Tomkies' major article on McGoohan entitled *Fame Will Never Make Me A Prisoner*. London's *TV Times* meanwhile promoted *Dance of the Dead* with an item called *Snapshots from the Village of Mystery* presenting four colour shots from *Arrival*.

On Monday 27 November, McGoohan and his team headed for Mayfield in Sussex to shoot location material at an abandoned railway tunnel next to the A267; other location work for *Fall Out* would take in the A1 and London Road near MGM. Work on the sound stages resumed on Tuesday 28 running through to Thursday 30 on inserts for both *Fall Out* and *The Girl Who Was Death*. Friday 1 December was then spent on a final location shoot at Beachy Head for *The Girl Who Was Death* … and *The Prisoner* had wrapped. Like many others, assistant director Gino Marotta recalled the relief of getting to the end of "One of the most demanding jobs I've ever had" as he commented to Steven Ricks on *The Prisoner in Conclusion* (TR7 Productions, 1994).

## 6: "I HOPE THE TAX MAN GETS YOU"

The race was now on to edit the last four episodes of *The Prisoner* for transmission. Noreen Ackland, who had joined the series during October to work on *Living in Harmony*, was initially assigned the complex task of assembling *Fall Out* and was subsequently assisted by Eric Boyd-Perkins once *The Girl Who Was Death* had been completed. Even with help from Ackland's husband, Richard Best, editing would still run well into 1968.

*The Prisoner gets a death sentence* announced Brian Dean of the *Daily Mail* on Thursday 30 November. The previous day, Lew Grade confirmed: "We have no plans to make a new series." An ITV official added "It is a first-class series, but it has been criticised for being hard to understand." Patrick McGoohan commented: "I am pleased at the reception *The Prisoner* has had. It stimulated contention. That is always a good thing and is what I aimed for."

The London *TV Times* (2-8 December 1967) promoted the listing of *Checkmate* with a photograph of the Psychiatrist and the Queen, and the earlier critical letter generated a supportive backlash in the *Viewerpoint* column. Under the title *Six To One*, William H Watts of Wembley wrote: 'I must spring to the defence of our prisoner who, in the great John Drake tradition, gives each week a fresh helping of action, suspense and intrigue, a triple combination reflected in very few other dramatic offerings of any medium [...] To Number 1 actor and author Pat McGoohan, full marks. And to Number 6 villager, keep your chin up; you are not alone in your weekly vigil.' His thoughts were echoed by H Conridge of London N4, whose missive commented: 'I consider *The Prisoner* the best series ever produced and one of the very few high spots of the week. As for Patrick McGoohan – Magnificent.' The fact that guest star Derren Nesbitt could be seen in both *The Prisoner* and *Man in a Suitcase* (the episode *Dead Man's Shoes*) that week earned the actor a feature in the *People* section of *TV World* (2-8 December 1967) to promote *It's Your Funeral*.

With *The General* on Friday 1 December, Granada's audience fell sharply to plateau at little over two million. The same week, overall performance of *The Prisoner* across the UK propelled it into TAM's National Top 20 for the only time; the cumulative effect of episodes like *Hammer into Anvil* and *Checkmate* saw the series claim twentieth position thanks to 5.9 million homes and *Checkmate* achieved tenth position on Southern.

On Friday 8 December, *It's Your Funeral* hit a 2.1 million peak in series ratings for ATV Midlands and Grampian. However, Sunday audiences had been declining following the Royal Command. Three striking paintings of McGoo-

*TV Tornado*: looking rather more like a homage to *Danger Man* than *The Prisoner*

*Daily Mail* (30 November 1967)

# The Prisoner gets a death sentence

### By BRIAN DEAN

INDEPENDENT Television's controversial adventure series *The Prisoner* will disappear in February.

It has been one of the most expensive series produced by British television.

Mr. Lew Grade, head of ATV Network, said yester-

han as *The Prisoner* graced the cover of the comic *TV Tornado* with Issue 48 (9 December 1967), but there was no other coverage for the 'cover man' inside. While *The Prisoner* had concluded its run in Canada, December saw it making its debut in New Zealand.

*Television Today* announced ATV's plans for the 1968 New Year season on Thursday 14 December, indicating that London would continue with *The Prisoner* on Sundays through to 4 February, after which it would be replaced by *The Saint* (actually repeats); thus the show would not air Christmas Eve. In the London *TV Times* (16-22 December 1967), the billing for *It's Your Funeral* was accompanied by a picture of Monique and her father.

On Monday 18 December, Mary Malone penned *No get out for The Prisoner's script men* for the *Daily Mirror*, noting the series' 'story is always the same' and the format's structure from the outset 'relies on McGoohan's failure'. To promote the series' foray into the Wild West, *TV World* (23-29 December 1967) had a feature about Frank Maher in its *People* section while the listing was accompanied by a shot of the 'Sheriff' with the Judge.

Without *The Prisoner* on Christmas Eve, Londoners saw the 1954 movie *Beau Brummell* while Southern and Westward aired the 1960 film *Ice Palace* and Tyne-Tees ran an edition of *Candid Camera*. In the final issue of *The Listener* for the year (28 December 1967), Anthony Burgess saw little to look forward to in 1968's television, apart from exceptions like '*The Prisoner*, which I'm sure is highly unpopular.' After the yuletide break, *A Change of Mind* attracted little over three million viewers to ATV London and its affiliates on New Year's Eve – over two million down from the show's peak.

1968 brought new schedules for some regions. Border screened *It's Your Funeral* as usual at 7.30pm on Thursday 28 December 1967, but in 1968 *A Change of Mind* appeared at 8pm on Friday 5 January. Similarly, *Do Not Forsake Me Oh My Darling* went out on Anglia at 8pm on Friday 29 December, followed by *Living in Harmony* at 7.35pm on Saturday 6 January.

There was a more serious scheduling issue for ATV Midlands and Grampian who were still leading the broadcasts, having aired *Living in Harmony* on Friday 29 December. *Fall Out* would not be ready to screen on Friday 19 January as hoped. To buy an extra fortnight, ATV Midlands (and Grampian) pulled forward their first broadcast of the two colour *Danger Man* episodes, provisionally scheduled for the two weeks following *Fall Out*. This had previously happened in early 1967 where transmission of the new colour episodes of *The Saint* caught up with filming, necessitating monochrome repeats from 1964/5 to be scheduled on alternate weeks. *TV World* (30 December 1967–5 January 1968) ran the article *Drake is back – and the pace Is Still Punishing*, explaining that Drake was replacing Number 6 for the next fortnight.

Ulster ran *The Prisoner* at 8.55pm on Saturdays starting on 6 January; the only region not running the series was Television Wales and West. A black and white shot of Number 6 from *Arrival* publicised the listing for *Do Not Forsake Me Oh My Darling* in the London *TV Times* (6-12 January 1968). From Sunday 7 January, Southern, Westward and Channel rescheduled *The Prisoner*; they screened movies in the early evening, recorded the ATV London transmission and relayed it at 10.05pm, leaving ATV London and Tyne Tees to maintain the primetime 7.25pm Sunday night slot. On BBC1, *Steptoe and Son* and *Ironside* had concluded; the regular replacement was the controversial CBS import *The Smothers Brothers Comedy Hour* which failed to make any impact on the ratings.

Patrick McGoohan and Roger Moore's status as producers of their own series (Moore being the co-owner of Bamore which made *The Saint*) was emphasised in *Variety* on Wednesday 3 January. In *The Guardian* on Friday 5, critic Keith Dewhurst's study of Rediffusion's drama *A Man of Our Times* noted that compromise affected all series, commenting 'The Prisoner [is] a too bizarre attempt to find a new inspiration'.

After *Living in Harmony*, Anglia also dropped *The Prisoner* for a fortnight, screening the 1955 movies *The Desperate Hours* and *Blood Alley*. The London *TV Times* (13-19 January 1968) emphasised the programme listing for *Living in Harmony* with a shot of the lead character on horseback, while in *TV World* (13-19 January 1968) features on guest artistes Justine Lord and John Drake helped promote *The Girl Who Was Death*.

By mid-January, *Fall Out* was completed and *The Prisoner* vanished from the MGM production lists on the week of Saturday 13 January. Portmeirion was again confirmed as the 'amazing "Continental" village from which (on TV) Patrick McGoohan is always trying to escape in *The Prisoner*' in a feature about holidaying in Wales in the *Daily Express* on Saturday 13.

McGoohan directs his guest cast on *Fall Out*

On Sunday 14 January, ratings in London and the South improved as *Living in Harmony* attracted just under five million viewers. Looking at the western in *Television Today* on Thursday 18, critic Angela Moreton titled her review *A lack of character and conviction*, declaring that it was 'All very puzzling, although to give the story […] its due, it was quite gripping.' She found the show 'faultlessly produced' although it 'had that machine-made conveyor belt quality that is the robber of individuality'.

The *Danger Man* fortnight meant ATV Midlands and Grampian no longer led the field. Scottish debuted *The Girl Who Was Death* on Thursday 18 January, broadcasting from videotape rather than film (presumably because the

35mm print was needed in the Midlands next day). *The Prisoner* was then back on ATV Midlands from Friday 19 January. By now, BBC1's Friday opposition was espionage adventure with *The Man from UNCLE* which let Number 6 have his head in the ratings. In London, a shot of Sonia and Number 6 accompanied the listing for *The Girl Who Was Death* in the *TV Times* (20-26 January 1968), while in *TV World* a monochrome shot of Number 6 and Number 2 emphasised *Once upon a Time*'s billing (20-26 January 1968).

'It's a very exciting finish.'
(Leo McKen on *Fall Out*)

Press attention grew as *The Prisoner* thundered towards its conclusion. On Sunday 21 January, the *Sunday Mirror* ran James Pettigrew's *McGoohan has the answer – to a mystery baffling millions* which looked at 'one of the most costly and controversial series ever made by ITV' and named the final episode as *Fall-out* [sic]. With the seventeen episodes having cost £850,000, the journalist pondered, 'Will the courageous Mr Grade make the bumper profit he hoped for from American and world sales, or will he just about break even?' That evening, *The Girl Who Was Death* rated tenth in London's TAM chart.

In Australia, *The Prisoner* debuted in Melbourne on Channel HSV7 at 8pm on Monday 22 January 1968. In the UK, ITC generated a document which attempted to answer the inevitable questions about *Fall Out*. This included interpretive statements like 'The Village could be the real and unconscious world of civilization today. We are all prisoners without bars.' Some questions were met with other questions in true McGoohan style, such as 'Is there no trust in the Village?: What has happened to trust among nations?' Other items were decidedly abstract; could science interpose into an individual's dreams: 'Number Six says no. The spirit of the individual is supreme. The possibility is haunting, though. How many Number Sixes are there in the world?'

*TV World* prepared readers for *Fall Out* with *Unmasking Day for Face of No. 1* (27 January–2 February 1968) which promised the identity of Number 1, with the caveat 'But watch closely, because he won't be served up to you on a platter.' Guest star Alexis Kanner told viewers, "This has been a big show which needs a big pay-off. And that's what you'll get." Leo McKern commented, "It's a very exciting finish. To say anything about it, would give the game away."

Asked if he was Number 1, tight-lipped Angelo Muscat said, "Whenever I'm recognised in the street, that's the first question I'm asked. No. I'm not saying whether it's true. That would spoil it." The programme billing for *Fall Out* was accompanied by a shot of the Butler.

The *Daily Mail*'s Peter Black commented on the forthcoming end of 'ATV's ambitious flop' on Friday 26 January. Erroneously claiming that the series had 'done badly in America', he added that it 'was sad to watch such style screwing itself into the ground every week, but McGoohan never mastered the difficult business of opening it out.'

Granada shifted slots slightly with *Living in Harmony* screened at the later time of 7.55pm on Friday 26 January, while Anglia resumed with *The Girl Who Was Death* on Saturday 27 January. Although the later episodes were clearly available for broadcast, Granada instigated a fortnight's break from *The Prisoner*, scheduling the US science-fiction series *The Invaders* on Friday 2 and Friday 9 February.

In the meantime, there were reported leaks of the series conclusion to the public. Kenneth Baily of *The People* managed to speak to McGoohan about the apparent disclosures, with the writer/director responding: "Reports alleging how it all ends are nothing near what viewers will see next Sunday. The real ending is diametrically opposed to the supposed leak of the ending."

*Fall Out* made its debut on Thursday 1 February courtesy of Scottish Television. Press coverage continued to blossom that day as *McGoohan is a prisoner of his imagination* by Fergus Cashin appeared in the *Daily Sketch*. 'A nut case I know is driving to friends in Birmingham tomorrow night to get the final solution at 7.30 on Midlands TV. He can't wait until Sunday,' wrote the journalist, noting that McGoohan had endured the public telling him that they liked *Danger Man* but could not understand *The Prisoner*. "I'm not at all annoyed," said the actor, "I love people. They are entitled to their views." McGoohan spoke of the CBS projects (*Brand* and "a massive historical epic for MGM plus a comedy and a western") and took the chance to state his beliefs: "Everything is force fed in one direction – beans, religion, the scar on the President's belly, the fingers on the button, Alf [Garnett from the BBC1 sitcom *Till Death Us Do Part*], No 6, No 10. Somebody needs to yell a warning. I hope I'm giving some kind of warning. My village is not 1984, but 1968 … MORE THAN ANYTHING ELSE I BELIEVE PASSIONATELY IN THE FREEDOM OF THE INDIVIDUAL. *I WANT TO YELL BACK: 'THAT'S OUR RIGHT. THE LOSS OF ONE'S OWN INDIVIDUALITY IS A NIGHTMARE.'* And if I haven't made my 'yell back' clear in *The Prisoner*, the individual viewer has the right to shout 'Nuts to you, Paddy boy'."

*TV Times* braced viewers in the south for the last episode of the 'most bizarre thriller series ever' with *Patrick McGoohan talks ...* by Anthony Davis (3-9 February 1968). Interviewed by phone while editing *Fall Out*, McGoohan

'Nuts to you, Paddy boy.' McGoohan faces controversy as *Fall Out* airs on ITV (below)

**7.25 The Prisoner**
STARRING
**PATRICK McGOOHAN**
*as The Prisoner*
IN
**Fall Out**
GUEST STARS
**LEO McKERN**
**KENNETH GRIFFITH**
**ALEXIS KANNER**
The Butler......... **Angelo Muscat**
The Supervisor..... **Peter Swanwick**
The Delegate....... **Michael Miller**
WRITTEN BY PATRICK McGOOHAN
SCRIPT EDITOR GEORGE MARKSTEIN
DIRECTED BY PATRICK McGOOHAN
PRODUCED BY DAVID TOMBLIN
EXECUTIVE PRODUCER
PATRICK McGOOHAN
At last the end of a nightmarish adventure is in sight. A trial determines the Prisoner's ultimate fate …
*ATV Network Presentation*

declared, "I've done a job. I set out to make a specific number of films. I've made them. The series has come to an end. It's just the end of a job, that's all. It was meant to be controversial and it has been. If it has failed in some respects it's a pity, but I don't think it has. Letters I've received have been fascinating. Some of them aren't at all complimentary but the pros outweigh the cons. Eleven million people watched it every week. What more do you want?" When asked if *Fall Out* would answer the series' many riddles, McGoohan replied "No, it doesn't" while an ITC spokesman claimed "The answers are there, in fact, but [...] not answered straight-forwardly at surface level." When asked if the show would return, McGoohan declared: "Definitely not." In London, *Fall Out*'s listing was accompanied by a shot of Number 2 being held before Number 6 and the Butler.

McGoohan was 'giving up making any more TV series' according to Martin Jackson in the *Daily Express* on Friday 2 February. "I have devoted enough of my life to television. I have had enough. I was asked to do 32 episodes of *The Prisoner* but to be honest I couldn't. I was so mentally and physically whacked," explained the actor who had completed 'the 16th episode' that week.

An estimated 2,500,000 Midlanders watched *Fall Out* on Friday 2 February; the next week, ATV Midlands replaced *The Prisoner* with 1965 re-runs of *The Saint*. The morning after Number 1 was revealed to Midland viewers, McGoohan spoke to Clifford Davis in the *Daily Mirror*, admitting in *The Prisoner confesses ...* "It has knocked me out. I'm whacked. Which is why I'm stopping. I just can't do any more." He admitted of the show "it hasn't come off 100 per cent." Aware the stories were baffling for viewers, he commented: "My own teenaged daughter was confused." Pinpointing shortcomings, he realised there was too little preparation, blaming the CBS pre-sale: "The progression of the story needed to be much more related to the original premise. We should have had a year's preparation. It was a great error to start with only five or six scripts. I should have had all the scripts before we started." Of the final episode he commented, "As far as I'm concerned it's explained. But I admit a great deal is still left open. [It's] an allegory. A fable. But I'm almost willing to bet you see the point to the final episode."

Southern offered *Fall Out* in the original primetime slot of 7.25pm from London, while it remained at 10.05pm on Westward and Channel. The Sunday transmission performed well, attracting six million viewers; the climax charted fourth in London (48) and sixth for both Tyne Tees (51) and Anglia (45) where it was shown the following week. With *The Prisoner* concluded, ATV London also reallocated the slot to 1962 reruns of *The Saint*.

The *Daily Telegraph*'s Peter Knight had initially been well disposed to the show, but his review on Monday 5 February was entitled *Angry Viewers left in dark on 'Prisoner'*. 'Within seconds of the credit titles appearing on the

Below and opposite: 'Mentally and physically whacked.' McGoohan directing *Fall Out*

screen, the switchboard at ATV House, Mayfair was jammed with calls from angry viewers. It was not until half an hour later that they were able to cope with the incoming calls,' related Knight. An ATV spokesman declared, "It is left up to the viewer to put his own interpretation on the story." McGoohan refused to give an explanation: "Why should I? It is their responsibility to put their own interpretation. I have certainly not held a shotgun at viewers' heads and forced them to watch the programme." The actor felt that the audience response was "the most marvellous thing that has happened to me in my life." Knight felt a charitable interpretation of *Fall Out*, 'was an illustration of an individual's fight to retain his own identity and personality against the regimentations of modern government and society.' However, despite 'production gloss, sophisticated writing and fine acting', the final impression was 'a heap of hokum carried off with all the smoothness of a confidence trick.'

The same day in *The Sun*, Richard Last bid *Farewell to the Prisoner – and no Regrets*, saying *The Prisoner* was a warning of allowing 'gimmickry

'Doing a bit of cerebral work.'
McGoohan directs on *Fall Out*

and camera technique for its own sake [to] take over from creative thinking.' Condemning the 'monstrously drawn-out' series, he felt the 'final "trial" sequences failed to explain anything and 'only compounded confusion.' In the *Daily Mail*, Barry Norman had watched *The Prisoner* from the start with 'admiration and bafflement.' He admired the series for introducing a 'deeper element' into a popular genre, and suspected a Sunday night audience disliked 'doing a bit of cerebral work.' Norman was stumped by McGoohan's message and declared the show as 'a commendable near-miss.' Elsewhere in the *Mail*, Denis Morris spoke to McGoohan in *It was my Vietnam, says 'Prisoner'*. "It was about the things which could lead to situations like Vietnam," explained the star, "I cannot explain it any more than I can the pictures from Vietnam which appear in the papers every day. You can only look at them and cry and pray." Of specific items, McGoohan explained that the penny-farthing was "Our progess – slow", the 'balloon' was "Bubble reputation", the rocket was "Where we might all end up" and the 'Little Butler' was "Whatever you want to make of him." Morris reported that 'Two dozen people rang up after last night's episode asking for an explanation.'

*Variety* announced on Wednesday 7 that *The Prisoner* was CBS' summer replacement for the new variety series *The Jonathan Winters Show* running at 10pm on Wednesdays. Back in the UK, in his editorial for *Television Today* on Thursday 8 February, Edward Durham Taylor's piece *Expensive failure but nothing to crow about* noted that the audience was 'feeling angry or cheated' over the ending, noting that the first two episodes had suggested that the show was 'nothing more than a succession of elaborate sets and unlikely to be anything more unless there was a remarkable improvement in the script and characterisation.' Questioning the wisdom of offering control to an inexperienced producer, Taylor commented that '*The Prisoner* leaves us with the impression that the ideas had never been worked out further than the basic idea.' In *Kinematograph Weekly* (10 February 1968), Tony Gruner celebrated *Prisoner justifies production costs*, noting that 'only a sponsor like Lew Grade [...] could have stood by a series when production costs jumped from £50,000 to £75,000 an episode.'

Prompted by *Fall Out*, the London *TV Times* printed letters in *Viewerpoint* (17-23 February) under the title *That prisoner*. Helena Smith of Dorchester wrote: 'Please thank Patrick McGoohan and the rest of the cast [...] We enjoyed the last episode as much as the first and were able to answer many of the questions posed during the series.' She understood the allegorical statement in which 'The Prisoner refused to conform to the pattern laid down by the Establishment, Bureaucracy, call it what you will [...] It made my family think and great credit is due to an actor who takes life seriously enough to live it his way.' Mrs Patricia M Rance of SW4 queried in verse: 'Woe is me! How can it be./That Patrick has gone mad?/For really I have never seen/A series quite so bad!/The final "thrilling" episode/I watched in disbelief./Trying to find some substance/Of a story underneath./I suppose *The Prisoner* stories/Are very clear to him,/They certainly are not clear to me./Am I a little dim?!!!' Referring to the outlandish Beatles film shown by BBC1 on Boxing Day, P.J. Nee of Great Missenden commented, 'I have come to the conclusion that it was part two of the *Magical Mystery Tour*'. 'I found it frightening, sometimes amusing and *always* disturbing,' admitted Miss G Richman of SW16 adding, 'I'm not much wiser after the final episode ... But even if the experiment did not quite succeed (and *I'm* sorry that it ended) I'd like to see more series or plays of this quality.'

The Midland audience's reactions were displayed in *TV World's Your View* (17-23 February 1968). Mrs Alice J Slack of Wimpstone declared, 'I feel compelled to say how much I enjoyed *The Prisoner*. Patrick McGoohan's capabilities are tremendous.' However, Mrs D E Cotton of Birmingham fumed, 'I hope I never see another series like *The Prisoner*. I have never seen anything so ridiculous.'

From Sunday 18 February, thirteen episodes of *Le Prisonnier* were screened at 6.50pm by ORTF2. Meanwhile news of the series finale filtered across the Atlantic as a bulletin appeared in *Variety* on Tuesday 20 under the title *What Did It All Mean? 'Prisoner' Comes to an End Still Hanging Over Cliff*. This reported how critics and public were 'baffled to the very last frame of ATV's most expensive and lavish serial'. Although not a ratings topper, the '$168,000 an episode sci-fi-spy serial [...] has been a regular talking point around the business'. Already sold to 24 countries (including, Iran, Thailand, Holland and Lebanon), the show was scheduled for the summer by CBS 'dispelling conjecture here that it would never get on the American screens'. The

## 'Prisoner' justifies production costs

DESPITE certain criticisms from the fourth estate and bewilderment on the part of many viewers, " The Prisoner " series has been a success. First of all it has made a lot of money for ITC, and In America it will be presented on CBS at a peak time. The show has also been sold throughout Europe and in Japan as well as this country where it received a top UK price.

**TELEVISION**
**by Tony Gruner**

" The Prisoner " was the most expensive television series ever made in this country. Production costs for the show at one point reached £75,000 an episode. On the other hand these costs were clearly shown on the screen and the series itself had a quality comparable to the best television films made in America. As a result of its success with CBS, Patrick McGoohan, creator, star and producer of the series, has been given backing for a three picture deal by the CBS network.

Many months ago when production started on " The Prisoner " a member of the unit said to me: " This show will be either the

biggest flop in the history of British television or its greatest success." By the most critical yardstick, audience reaction, it has not flopped. Viewers have been annoyed and exasperated, but the younger generation has stuck with McGoohan and his show through...

*Kinematograph Weekly*
(10 February 1968)

*Variety* (20 February 1968)

## What Did It All Mean? 'Prisoner' Comes to An End Still Hanging Over Cliff

London, Feb. 20.

Critics and public alike remained baffled to the very last frame of ATV's most expensive and lavish serial, the Patrick McGoohan starrer, "The Prisoner," which ended its run here last week.

Now the rest of the world will have a chance to try and figure out what McGoohan had in mind when he devised his $168,000 an episode sci-fi-spy serial, which although it has not been a top ratings winner here, has been a regular talking point around the business during its 17-part run.

To date ATV has sold the series to 24 countries, including the U.S., where CBS has set it for summer screening thus dispelling con-

article filed in London described the show as 'Technically [...] probably the most dazzling [series] ever screened in this country' which while escaping 'the usual spy thriller rut' ended with an episode which 'left everybody more bewildered than ever and irritated many sufficiently for the net's switchboard to be jammed by mystified callers demanding an explanation'. With McGoohan refusing to explain, the journalist reported that most saw it as the star expressing 'his personal protest against the increasing regimentation of the individual by modern society'. *Brand* was to film in Norway, with the first of the ATV/CBS projects to shoot from mid-June. Two days later, *The Times* noted that McGoohan was backing Kenneth Griffith's documentaries about Cecil Rhodes and relief of Mafeking.

The series climax left regular viewer Anthony Burgess cold in *The Listener* (22 February 1968), having been delighted that a meaning would emerge in the series as 'a kind of image of a single controlling imagination [...] We all had a right [...] for a final resolution which should satisfy on all levels. What we got was [...] especially appalling because of its typically pop mixture of the banal and pretentious.' Burgess felt that *Fall Out* 'put the onus of interpretation on the viewer and yet offered him nothing worthy of interpretation' and noted that he felt sad – rather than angry – because 'so much talent had been wasted. Later I reflected that the talent could only, after all, have been of the most superficial kind – the technical kind. There had been no imagination large enough to encompass so ambitious a conception.'

The initial *Fall Out* correspondence was the tip of the iceberg for *TV World*. The following week (24 February–1 March 1968), most of the *Your View* page was devoted to *The Prisoner* under the title *WHO really was No. 1?* McGoohan explained to readers: 'Number One is the worst part of one's self. Number One made Hitler. Get rid of Number One and we are free.' The viewers then had their say. 'The final episode of *The Prisoner* was terrible,' declared Miss D Broadhurst of Westfields, 'Surely Patrick McGoohan should have more sense than to write and produce such a ridiculous programme.' 'I've never seen such nonsense rubbish and the final episode was the daddy of them all,' wrote Mrs B A Rea of Lichfield. 'The most incoherent rubbish I have ever watched,' said Kenneth Green of Kings Norton, while Mrs Doreen E Walker of Nuneaton asked, 'Why did No. 6 resign? The last two episodes were utter rubbish.' 'I watched carefully, as you advised. I am as wise now as I was at the beginning of the series,' wrote Mrs E M Baldock of Nuneaton, adding, 'I trust that Patrick McGoohan feels much better now?' 'My husband and I are normal, intelligent people, but we were completely baffled,' said Mrs Patricia Bradley of Jacksdale. However, Graham Stafford of Birmingham wrote 'Congratulations to Patrick McGoohan. The final episode was an absolutely brilliant piece of surrealism.'

The internal *ATV Newsheet* Vol 8 No 2 (February 1968) noted that 'During and immediately after the London transmission [...] the ATV Duty

Above: ATV attempts to explain *Fall Out,* below and opposite. Opposite below: Local service only... Dinky Toys' die-cast Mini Moke

Office logged well over 150 calls – in the main from a confused public. The following day, the mail began to flood in. Strangely enough, the trends of the previous evening were reversed with a heavy correspondence in favour of the series.' A staff writer then attempted to explain some of the imagery, examples being 'The Village: It does not exist in any materialistic form. It symbolised the prison that is man's own mind […] The Balloon – Rover: Symbolises repression and the guardianship of corrupt authority which, when corruption is finally overcome, disintegrates […] No.1: The unveiling of No.1 as Patrick McGoohan himself is representative of every man's desire to be No.1 – to be the top dog.'

ATV and MGM responded to viewer correspondence by mailing out signed photographs of the cast and also Number 6 badges. In February 1968, Dinky – who had enjoyed success with die-cast toys based on vehicles from *Thunderbirds* – released a variation of an existing Moke die-cast toy from 1966 as *The Prisoner* Mini Moke model 106; this was discontinued by 1970. The model was promoted by Chris Jelley in *Meccano Magazine* (February 1968) as he commented that 106 was 'a tremendously appealing model'.

Finally, Granada viewers saw what the fuss was about as *The Prisoner* resumed at 7.55pm on Friday 23 February, with *Fall Out* the following week. Ulster decided that *The Prisoner* was not a post-watershed series and swapped it in the schedules with *Man in a Suitcase* meaning that *Dance of the Dead* found itself in the 8pm slot on Friday 23 February.

Adam Hopkins of the *Sunday Times* spoke to McGoohan about the series in *How the escaped Prisoner will get a new Brand image* (25 February 1968). "I had a lovely letter from a smashing feller, a colonel, you know, Order of the British Empire," commented the star, "'Sir,' he said, 'I've watched ten of them now and I've never seen such an utter load of tripe. I wish to say unreservedly that if nothing else happens to you, I hope the tax man gets you.' I wrote back thanking him for his interest and hoping he'd stick it out for six more programmes."

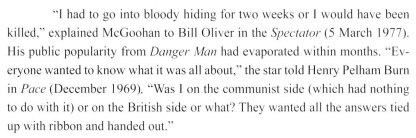

'The poor twerp...' *The Prisoner* spoofed in *Smash* comic, (2 March, 1968)

"I had to go into bloody hiding for two weeks or I would have been killed," explained McGoohan to Bill Oliver in the *Spectator* (5 March 1977). His public popularity from *Danger Man* had evaporated within months. "Everyone wanted to know what it was all about," the star told Henry Pelham Burn in *Pace* (December 1969), "Was I on the communist side (which had nothing to do with it) or on the British side or what? They wanted all the answers tied up with ribbon and handed out."

"I hoped that there would be a bit of an outcry," said McGoohan in 1983. "I knew there would be something going on, because it wasn't the conventional ending. [The audience] still had this idea that it was a secret agent story." In *Six into One*, he ventured: "A lot of people watched the last episode and expected a conventional end with the evil person personified as the Number 1 character that brooded over everything. They expected a more sort of James Bond villain. I think they felt robbed with what they got. I would argue against that. I don't think they were robbed. It was an allegory [...] You can't expect it to end like James Bond, so you have an allegorical ending."

Issue 109 of the comic *Smash!* placed Number 6 in the *Charlie's Choice* strip drawn by Brian Lewis (2 March 1968). Charlie owned a 'TV set with a difference' where characters came to life; while watching *The Prisoner*, Charlie commented, "I feel sorry for the poor twerp! I think I'll get him free!" Falling from the screen onto his head, Number 6 was then terrified of Charlie's bubble gum blowing which he feared was "that fiendish bubble thing".

For his fortieth birthday, McGoohan took a break in Switzerland with his family. In addition to Griffith's documentary and *Brand* (adapted by David Tomblin and Terence Feely), other projects lined up for Everyman included an adaptation of Leon Garfield's period novel *Black Jack* by Terence Feely, the US cavalry period piece *When Trumpets Call* by Charles K Peck Jnr and *The Soldier*, about a retired mercenary in Rural Ireland being forced back into action. Feely recalled to David Richardson in *TV Zone* Issue 46 (September 1993): "Something went wrong [...] Lew's money was withdrawn."

Ulster ratings were not good and from *Living in Harmony* on Friday 5 April, *The Prisoner* was relegated to 10.50pm, but reprieved to 8pm for *Fall Out* on Friday 26 April. Visitors at Portmeirion in 1968 shot from 10,000 per year to 100,000 per year, and when ATV got the Queen's Award for Industry for outstanding achievements in the field of exports, the *ITA: Annual Report and Accounts 1967-68* cited *The Prisoner* as part of that success, noting 'it is regrettable that it had to be shown here in monochrome, rather than the original colour in which it was made.'

# 7: "METAPHYSICAL OBSERVATIONS AND QUICKSILVER IMAGERY"

n the USA *The Prisoner* had been ear-marked as a summer replacement for one of CBS' regular programmes, and on Thursday 11 April *Variety* revealed that it would now deputise for the popular comedy sketch vehicle *The Jackie Gleason Show*, at 7.30pm on Saturdays from 1 June. 'This is no routine British whodunit, but a controversial TV series that brought screams of anguish and dismay when it was shown in England this past season [...] The screams came from viewers and critics at the enigma of it all,' wrote Joan Barthel in her four page article *An Enigma Comes to American TV* in *TV Guide* (25-31 May 1968), illustrated by an eye-catching shot from *Free For All*. The following week (1-7 June 1968), CBS ran half-page adverts in the listings with a moody close-up of Patrick McGoohan to get viewers tuning into the ITC offering while *Arrival* was emphasised as a highlighted programme with another photograph of its star. 'The *Secret Agent* theme wailed, "They've given you a number and taken away your name." In this series it happens,' declared the *Close-up* box-out, 'You'll have to shake your imagination to guess why [...] The series, produced in England, uses lavish sets, dramatic technical effects and quick-cut camera techniques.'

CBS broadcast *The Prisoner* in colour, with an additional commercial break, plus specially assembled trailers narrated by David Healy enticing viewers to tune in next week. The Saturday slot placed it up against *The Dating Game* and *The Newlywed Game* on ABC, and reruns of *The Saint* on NBC, and also meant that some affiliated stations would pre-empt the show for live football coverage. Paul Henniger penned *Prisoner Arrives on CBS* for the *LA Times* on Monday 3 June, commenting of the series 'perhaps McGoohan has some encouraging words for us in the last one.' He feared that '*The Prisoner* has arrived too late for an audience that's been brainwashed with such James-Bond-Man From UNCLE goings-on for years' but 'should provide some interesting summer hours.' Lawrence Laurent's *The Prisoner: a Promising New Series* in the *Washington Post* described the show as an 'action-adventure series about a loser', noting that US viewers were 'conditioned to simple cause-and-effect stories about all-conquering heroes.' With 'scenic beauty' and 'gloss of production', the show was compared to Orwell's *1984* as Laurent pondered: 'So, who is *The Prisoner*? He could be anyone of us.' Bill of *Variety* also looked at the CBS debut of the 'eerie, *1984* type of suspenser [which] may be too strong for some, but it packs a potent punch.' While the plot was sometimes 'blurry and could have had more exposition', the show was 'arrest-

US listings magazine *TV Guide* welcomes *The Prisoner* (1–7 June, 1968)

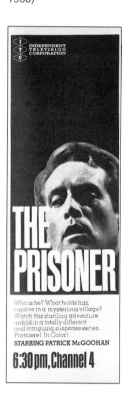

ing' and 'hardhitting and, in fact, may be too much for those viewers accustomed to the antics of Jackie Gleason, normally in this time slot.'

Meanwhile, McGoohan was still in Switzerland and so did not attend a Ministry of Housing inquiry at Hendon Town Hall on Thursday 13 June to discuss a six foot high screen which he had erected around his Mill Hill home to protect the privacy of his family from photographers.

In the US, *The Chimes of Big Ben* had been scheduled for Saturday 8 June but was postponed for coverage of the funeral of Senator Robert Kennedy following his assassination on Wednesday 5. The deferred episode then aired in place of *A. B. and C.* on Saturday 15, which in turn replaced the advertised *Free For All* on Saturday 22. When Jack Gould of the *New York Times* looked at CBS' schedules on Monday 17, he commented of the 'lavishly produced exercise in obscurity' that 'Mr McGoohan requires a viewer to work as hard as he does.' *Variety* reported Puerto Rica buying the show on Wednesday 19, and *Time Magazine* featured the article *The Private I* on Friday 21, commenting that 'McGoohan regards *The Prisoner* as a protest against "the dehumanizing, the 'numeralization,' the loss of individuality which is happening to us all" – a thought that […] is fast becoming a benumbing cliché.' The 'supercool Briton' was currently somewhere in Switzerland; unlike Number 6, 'McGoohan has succeeded in preserving his privacy.' Generally, the feeling was that because of 'downbeat endings and murky symbolism [...] CBS has scheduled the series only as a June-September filler'.

*Free For All* aired on Saturday 29 June, followed by *The Schizoid Man* and *The General*. On Tuesday 2 July *Variety* announced that McGoohan was to play the title role in James Clavell's *Tai-Pan*, the first of his two films for MGM/ Filmways; a few weeks later on Wednesday 14 August the paper indicated shooting was soon to start at Elstree. In the *Washington Post* on Tuesday 16 July, Lawrence Laurent's view of summer television noted that '*The Prisoner* is welcome […] Viewers are supposed to argue about the true meaning […] and decide that McGoohan is trying to warn us of the perils of conformity and the loss of human individuality [but after] a half dozen episodes the point tends to get frazzled.' For Laurent, the show was saved by its 'superb production' and McGoohan's performance. Meanwhile in the UK, the *Daily Mail* reported on Tuesday 16 that McGoohan had been staying at Vevey on the banks of Lake Geneva and was thinking of relocating his family there permanently from Mill Hill.

'*The Prisoner* is the best thing to happen to television in a long time. It is sophisticated, thoughtful, unique. When is it going to be canceled?' wrote

Cynthia Holtz of Far Rockaway, New York in the *Letters* section of *TV Guide* (20-26 July 1968), while elsewhere in the issue *Many Happy Returns* was emphasized by a *Close-up* box. The editor replied that 'Only 17 episodes were purchased, the last will be seen in September.' With *The Jackie Gleason Show* due to return on Saturday 28 September for the Fall season, the one-week preemption meant that one episode of *The Prisoner* would not be airing on CBS. The missing show would be the atypical *Living in Harmony*. According to *The Official Prisoner Companion* by Matthew White and Jaffer Ali (Warner Books, 1988), 'spokesmen for both CBS and ITC are on the record as saying that the Vietnam issue killed the episode', suggesting that it was Number 6's refusal to carry a gun in the episode that went against the contemporary US Army Draft.

Various local papers revealed the true location of the Village, such as Clay Gowran's *It's a Bizarre North Wales Beauty Spot* in the *Chicago Tribune* on Friday 26 July. After *Dance of the Dead* on Saturday 27 July, the intended UK order was adopted by CBS, with *Do Not Forsake Me Oh My Darling* airing on Saturday 3 August and being blessed with a *TV Guide Close-up*. This was followed by *It's Your Funeral, Checkmate, A Change of Mind* and *Hammer into Anvil* through to Friday 31 August. In *TV Guide* (31 August – 6 September 1968), acclaimed SF novelist Isaac Asimov penned the article *Hitch Your Wagon To A Rock*, speculating that the Prisoner's full name was Theodore Prisoner. In *Arrival*, Asimov expected the hero to escape and felt Number 6 was a failure. However, his thirteen year-old daughter explained to him, 'McGoohan is trying to portray the plight of modern man trapped in a conventional society that he is incapable of altering and yet from which he cannot escape,' allowing the writer to understand that *The Prisoner* was popular because it cracked the 'folly of success'.

'The network decision-makers objected to the frustration level of *The Prisoner*, asking McGoohan for greater tolerance of the sensibilities of viewers,' noted the *Saturday Review* (7 September 1968) describing the show as 'something innovative that has significant implications for the future of action-adventure TV entertainment.' That evening *The Girl Who Was Death* aired, followed by *Once upon a Time* on Saturday 14. The sequence concluded on Saturday 21 September with *Fall Out*, described by *TV Guide* in its *Close-up* feature as 'a razzle-dazzle display of metaphysical observations and quicksilver imagery.' The same issue's *Letter* section carried a missive from Christine Neibert of Englewood, Ohio: 'And so as *The Prisoner* slowly sinks into the murky depths of Situation Sea, we leave the bright land of imaginative TV and with a heartfelt farewell to that rare and wonderful No.6 we can only say "We knew it was too good to last."'

In the aftermath of the CBS screening, Clay Gowran penned *McGoohan's Series Still a Puzzle* in the *Chicago Tribune* on Friday 1 November, drawing upon answers provided by ITC's Murray Horowitz concerning the Village ('represents civilisation today. We're all prisoners without bars'), the

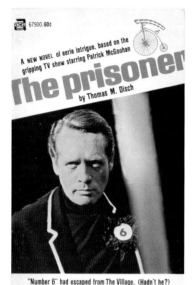

"Number 6" had escaped from The Village. (Hadn't he?)
Then why was he imprisoned there again? (Or was he?)

Thomas M. Disch attempts to undo the events of *Fall Out* in Ace Books' first *Prisoner* novel

'balloon' ('symbolic repression of human will') and the 'fat little butler' ('the little man of every community, prepared to follow faithfully').

While *Tai-Pan* was still in preparation during October, Patrick McGoohan and David Tomblin were preparing two British movies starring McGoohan to be made by Everyman in 1969, while ITC had nine films lined up including *Brand* (in February) and *The Mercenary* for CBS. In November 1968, Peter Swanwick died of a heart complaint aged only 46, his life already prolonged by major surgery in 1959.

McGoohan was announced as travelling to New York for the premiere of *Ice Station Zebra* on Friday 20 December. At the start of 1969, Richard Doan's *The Doan Report* in *TV Guide* (18 January 1969) noted that 'Viewers liked [*The Prisoner*] and complained when it was dropped. Some also thought that CBS callously ended the series without a denouement.' He added that CBS was planning repeats.

At a West Coast science-fiction convention, underground newspaper editor and filmmaker Henry Stein (who wrote as Hank Stine), suggested novels of *The Prisoner* to Terry Carr, editor of Ace Books which had enjoyed success since August 1965 with tie-in paperbacks for *The Man from UNCLE*. On the strength of his May 1968 novel *Camp Concentration,* writer Thomas M Disch was commissioned to continue where *Fall Out* finished. Number 6 bought a home in Wales, was kidnapped on a train, waking in the Village with no memory of his previous spell there. Breaking out, he returned to London and his old colleagues in a re-enactment of *Many Happy Returns*. Recaptured, his dreams were explored by Number 14, and he finally fled the Village having revealed an elderly woman cyborg to be Number 1. With a colour cover photograph from *Free For All, The Prisoner* was published Monday 7 April 1969.

In Japan, *The Prisoner* appeared on NHK from Sunday 2 March 1969. Back in the UK, ITC film series were good rerun material for ITV stations. The first region to schedule repeats was Granada, placing Number 6 around 2pm on Sunday afternoons from 13 April 1969. The original UK order was largely followed, although *Living in Harmony* succeeded *The Girl Who Was Death* with the Western placed at 11.10pm on the Saturday night schedule around the moon landing, before the series returned to Sundays, wrapping with *Fall Out* on 3 August.

CBS exercised their option to repeat *The Prisoner*, slotted in at 8pm on Thursdays in

place of the now-cancelled *The Jonathan Winters Show*. From 22 May to 11 September, the same sixteen shows were screened in the same order as 1968. Promoting *The Chimes of Big Ben*, *Time Magazine* (23 May 1969) commented, 'Those who missed the antics of imprisoned hero Patrick McGoohan [...] can catch the series this year.' Horowitz' 'Speculative Guide to the Prisoner' fuelled various local news articles such as *'Prisoner' Reruns Give Viewers 2d Chance To Fathom McGoohan* by Julia Inman in the *Indianapolis Star* (8 June 1969) while the *Washington Post* carried a full-page advert image from *Free For All* proclaiming '*The Prisoner* Is Back' on Sunday 15 June.

Back in the UK, since the original transmission of *The Prisoner*, in July 1968, the ITV franchises had been reallocated. TWW never screened *The Prisoner* in the west, but now HTV scheduled it on its split region, HTV West serving the Bristol area, at 10.30pm from Monday 7 July to 27 October 1969. Germany took thirteen episodes on ZDF as *Nummer Sechs* from Saturday 16 August 1969, and Jun Nagai's Japanese translation of Disch's novel appeared that month as #3228 of Hayakawa's Science Fiction Series. *Fall Out* was nominated for a Hugo Award as Best Dramatic Presentation at the 27th World Science Fiction Convention at the end of August 1969, but was beaten by *2001: A Space Odyssey*. Meanwhile, McGoohan was embarking on his second Hollywood film, MGM/Filmway's comedy drama *The Moonshine War* which started shooting on Monday 25 August through to mid-November.

Ace's second paperback, *The Prisoner #2* by David McDaniel, appeared on Monday 6 October with a cover shot from *Arrival*. Number 6 again awoke in the Village, this time with his car (KAR1260) which he then remodelled as a boat in an abortive attempt to escape out to sea. In the UK, Westward repeated *The Prisoner* at 11pm on Thursdays from 18 December running through to 23 April 1970 with transmissions relayed to Channel.

*The Prisoner* finally came to Portmeirion at 3.25pm on Wednesdays from 7 January 1970 with a haphazard afternoon run by HTV Wales through to Monday 27 April, omitting *Living in Harmony* which was now only scheduled post-watershed. The main ITV regions had started operating a colour service on Saturday 15 November 1969; the first company to air *The Prisoner* in colour was ATV (now serving only the Midlands), screening it at 11pm on Thursday nights from 12 February 1970 through to 2 July. Anglia reruns came next around 11pm on Thursdays from 6 August through to 26 November. In mid-November, MGM announced that *Tai-Pan* had been cancelled.

From May 1969, ITC had marketed all seventeen episodes of *The Prisoner* for US syndication and by February 1970 the series was appearing from stations such as

Two more novels from Ace Books

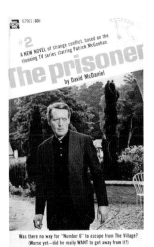

Was there no way for "Number 6" to escape from The Village?
(Worse yet—did he really WANT to get away from it?)

"Number 6" had a chance
to destroy the Village—
if that was really possible...

KTLA in Los Angeles. Including *Living in Harmony* in its run, the programme often appeared in off-peak slots and over the next few years would be screened from a variety of 16mm prints, including early edits of *Arrival* and *The Chimes of Big Ben*. Monday 1 June 1970 saw Ace produce their final paperback, *The Prisoner #3: A Day in the Life* by Hank Stine (later Jean Marie Stine) with a cover shot from *The Chimes of Big Ben*. In this, Number 6 (identified as Drake) was accused of hiding drugs, sentenced to death and then used by the Village authorities to kill off the three people who comprised Number 1 with characters from *Do Not Forsake Me Oh My Darling*.

New Year's Day 1971 saw Southern bringing Number 6 back to their screens at 11.10pm initially on Friday nights, concluding on Thursday 20 May. It then appeared on Tyne Tees at 11pm on Mondays from 13 September 1971 to 17 January 1972; the new London weekend channel LWT at 11.30pm on Fridays from 17 September 1971 to 7 January 1972 (apart from *Living in Harmony* and *The Girl Who Was Death*); and then Scottish, beginning at 11.15pm on Saturdays from 16 October to 27 November 1971, continuing in a haphazard manner at 11.05pm on Thursdays from 9 December through to 9 March 1972.

Meanwhile, McGoohan took a prominent role in the historical film *Mary, Queen of Scots* which began filming in Scotland and England on Monday 17 May 1971. His next two projects – *Queen Isabella* in 1972 and a version of the SF novel *Dune*, planned to film from March 1973 failed to materialise. Instead he directed the *Othello*-inspired rock opera *Catch My Soul* which filmed at Santa Fe in New Mexico from Monday 18 September 1972. Back in the UK, this time as a single region combining Wales and West, HTV screened *The Prisoner* for a second time at around 11.25pm on Saturdays from 15 April through to 12 August 1972.

On Wednesday 21 August 1974, it was announced that Everyman Films – and its directors Patrick McGoohan, David Tomblin and John Gambles – was bankrupt with debts of £62,916 and assets of only £517. Much of the debt was due to income tax on directors' earnings and the liquidation of McGoohan's other company, Drummond Enterprises, on Monday 30 November 1970.

Replacing Edward Asner at short notice, McGoohan – now resident in California – guest starred in *By Dawn's Early Light*, an instalment of the NBC detective series *Columbo* which was filmed in August 1974 and screened on Sunday 27 October. Meanwhile, *Il Prigioniero* made its Italian debut on RAI2 on Monday 11 November 1974.

Having filmed linking sequences to allow two episodes of Hammer's *Journey to the Unknown* anthology to be linked as *Journey into Darkness* for syndication, McGoohan took a role in the comedy western *The Genius* (aka *Un genio, due compari, un pollo*) which was filmed in Spain and the USA from Monday 24 March 1975; in May 1975, he won an Emmy for Best Single Performance (Supporting Actor) in *By Dawn's Early Light*. McGoohan then guested in another *Colombo* episode – *Identity Crisis* – which he also directed in August 1975 for broadcast on Sunday 2 November, after which he then directed a further instalment – *Last Salute to the Commodore* – during January 1976 for transmission on Sunday 2 May. Following this, McGoohan was cast as the villain in a new comedy film, *The Silver Streak* [sic], which started filming on Monday 12 April 1976.

Over summer 1976, McGoohan was planning to write and direct *Ponzi* (aka *The Boston Swindler*) which was to star Peter Falk, the star of *Columbo*. He was then cast in *The Man in the Iron Mask*, an NBC/ITC television movie to be filmed in France and at Twickenham Studios from the end of July 1976 for transmission in the New Year. Meanwhile, *The Prisoner* was starting a second lease of life …

Having purchased the comic strip rights to the series, Marvel Comics were also looking at a comic of *The Prisoner* for November 1976. Editor Marv Wolfman originally planned to write this himself, and an artist was lined up in the form of Gil Kane. However, Wolfman then passed the scripting onto Steve Englehart – a devotee of the series – with layouts by Joe Stanton. Following a fall out between Englehart and Marvel, the adaptation of *Arrival* was transferred to Jack Kirby whose seventeen pages also went unprinted when publisher Stan Lee felt the title did not fit his range.

By 1976, *The Prisoner* was worthy of serious study, and in Canada the Ontario Educational Communications Authority published *The Prisoner Puzzle* by Susan Nobel and Diana Goldsborough and *The Prisoner Program Guide* to promote discussion of repeats on TV Ontario; scheduled from Friday 1 October, in mid-September it was announced that these would be accompanied by editions of *The Prisoner Puzzle* presented by broadcaster Warner Troyer.

Television was now old enough as a medium to offer a sense of nostalgia. In the Midlands, ATV tapped into this with *Play It Again*, nine reruns of classic American film series including *Rawhide, The Fugitive, Maverick* and *77 Sunset Strip* which appeared on Saturday evenings from 1 May 1976. This generated a lot of interest in television from the 1950s and 1960s in the local press, further fuelled by the networked *Command Performance* of archive television at 10.30pm on Tuesdays from 29 June (including *77 Sunset Strip, Bonanza, Dr Kildare* and *Wagon Train*). Then on Saturday 10 July 1976, the *Birmingham Evening Mail* reported that *The Prisoner* would be returning to ATV soon …

'Best of luck with your exams.' Canadian academics deem *The Prisoner* worthy of study in 1976

The third UK screening of *The Prisoner* commenced on ITV via ATV at 11pm on Thursday 26 August … and it was this airing which would capture the imagination of viewers most strongly as the new genre of 'cult TV' began to emerge. Following 1976, the ongoing fascination with the series would fuel worldwide repeats, commercial releases, novels, comics, educational courses, appreciation societies, conventions, pop music, media coverage, computer games, spoofs, documentaries, soundtracks, remakes, books, stage plays, part-works, websites and countless other off-shoots in numerous media …all way beyond the scope and scale encompassed by this text which focuses only on its original period of creation and distribution.

Fifty years after its original broadcast, when the vast back catalogue of the quality film series distributed by ITC from the 1950s to the 1980s is studied, *The Prisoner* is still remarkably different ... to the extent that even individual episodes from the series offer sharp contrasts in tone, content and genre. Many ATV-backed shows fell into recognisable genres: swashbucklers, comedy misadventures, gritty crime and espionage, exotic continental escapades, life-saving Supermarionation heroics, charismatic philanthropists, outlandish alien adventure or simple hokum. But *The Prisoner* refused to be pushed, filed, stamped, briefed or debriefed as any of these categories. And throughout, it was dominated and directed by the vision of one man who had massive impact on both sides of the camera. And five decades of ripping up the rule book for adventure television, it remains breathtakingly different as a series which pushed the mix of genres to their very limits with massively enjoyable and memorable results. Thus, such a legacy has been bestowed on *The Prisoner* and its important status in the field of popular culture: it is a colourful, potent example of one of the earliest pieces of 'art' to emerge from the medium of television as it explored its boundaries in the innovative decade of the 1960s.

# 8: "PEOPLE LIKE A MYSTERY"

n 1967, television was considered as a largely disposable medium of instant entertainment. *The Prisoner* was made for a single primetime screening and then destined for obscurity like so many of its contemporaries. But fifty years later, its appeal continues to fascinate audiences new and old. "People like a mystery," observed Patrick McGoohan in 1983, "and I suppose that it is the sort of thing where a thousand people might have a different interpretation of it, which I think is very gratifying. I am glad that's the way it was, because that was the intention." Although this landmark series was the product of many people, conclusions about *The Prisoner* should be left with the man who steered the programme from conception to conclusion as one of television's first pieces of 'art': Patrick McGoohan:

"I had the chance to do something as nutty as I did. A chance that might come only once in a lifetime. If I was an idiot, so be it." (Alain Carrazé & Hélène Oswald, *Le Prisonnier: chef-d'oeuvre télévisionnaire*, 1989)

"It was a splash of objection on a canvas. It was an attempt – that failed, really – to try a slightly different type of television series and at the same time take a stand on something I feel very strongly about: numeralisation, mediocrity, this levelling of people by acceptance, it seems to me that part of rebellion today is the rebellion against acceptance." (Henry Pelham Burn, *Pace*, December 1969)

"I tried first of all to create a first-class piece of entertainment. I hope it rings true because here, too, I was concerned with the preservation of individual history […] If I have any kind of drum to beat in my life it is the drum of the individual. I believe that to be truly an individual, mentally clear and free, requires the greatest possible effort. And I seek this individuality in everything I do – in my work and in my private life. It's not easy. I am an actor first, although I'm now going into directing, producing and writing too. I find all these challenges, this total involvement, the most exciting way to live." (Mike Tomkies, *TV World*, 25 November–1 December 1967)

"The thing I remember most about it was hard work. So much hard work I didn't get much time to spend with my family." (Roger Goodman, April 1979)

"I'm happy to say that I was pleased with the overall production." (Barrington Calia, *New Video*, July 1985)

*"The Prisoner* was an allegorical conundrum ... It didn't have an answer." (*Time Out New York*, 24 July 1996)

"If I gave all the answers you would no longer have a role when watching it, although, yes, I could give you a precise answer to every part of the allegory." (Tim O'Sullivan, *Observer* Magazine, 15 December 1991)

"*The Prisoner* started as an experiment and became something of a cult." (Jane Oddy, *TV Week*, 21 October 1995)

"The greatest compliment I could possibly receive is for people to debate the meaning of it and I think that, probably, is why it has lasted so long, you know – that is very gratifying." (*Destination Serié*, October 1997)

"I don't want to do it again. I've done it. I want to go on." (Bill Oliver, *Spectator*, 5 March 1977)

"Once it's over, once I'd edited and delivered the last show, it's too late to do any more about it and I'd just as soon let the work, if it can be called that, stand by itself. But it keeps cropping up, [rearing] its ugly head." (*Simon Bates*, BBC Radio 1, 17 October 1990)

"It's going to take the rest of my life to live down *Danger Man* and *The Prisoner*." (*TV Times*, 18-24 January 1986)

"When will I be rid of this thing? I am the prisoner of *The Prisoner*." (Tim O'Sullivan, *Observer* Magazine, 15 December 1991)

# SELECT BIBLIOGRAPHY AND FURTHER READING

Booth, Rupert. *Not a Number: Patrick McGoohan – a life.* Supernova Books, 2011.

Britton, Piers D and Simon J Barker. *Reading Between Designs: Visual Imagery and the Generation of Meaning in The Avengers, The Prisoner and Doctor Who.* University of Texas Press, 2003.

Carrazé, Alain & Hélene Oswald. Trans. Christine Donougher. *The Prisoner: A Televisionary Masterpiece.* W.H. Allen & Co/Virgin, 1990.

Cook, John R & Peter Wright (eds). *British Science Fiction Television: A Hitchhiker's Guide.* IB Tauris, 2006. inc: 'Countering the counterculture: *The Prisoner* and the 1960s' by Sue Short.

Davies, Steven Paul. *The Prisoner Handbook.* Boxtree, 2002.

Davy, Rick. *The Prisoner: The Essential Guide.* Quoit Media, 2017.

Fairclough, Robert. *The Prisoner: the official companion to the classic TV series.* Carlton Books, 2002.

Fairclough, Robert (ed). *The Prisoner: The Original Scripts – Volume 1.* Reynolds and Hearn, 2005.

Fairclough, Robert (ed). *The Prisoner: The Original Scripts – Volume 2.* Reynolds and Hearn, 2006.

Frumerman, Catherine Németh. *On the Trail of The Prisoner.* PrizBiz, 2003.

Gregory, Chris. *Be Seeing You ... Decoding the Prisoner.* University of Luton Press, 1997.

Goodman, Roger (ed). *George Markstein and the Prisoner*. pandqmedia, 2014.

Johnson, Catherine. *Telefantasy*. BFI Publishing, 2005. inc: 'Serious Entertainment: *The Prisoner* and British Television in the 1960s'.

Langley, Roger. *The Prisoner in Portmeirion*. Portmeirion Limited, 1999.

Langley, Roger. *Patrick McGoohan: Danger Man or Prisoner?* Tomahawk Press, 2007.

Langley, Roger. *The Making of The Prisoner*. Escape, 2010.

Langley, Roger. *50 Years of The Prisoner*. Escape, 2016.

Mival, Eric. *Cutting Edge: My Life in Film and Television*. Quoit Media, 2016.

Rakoff, Ian. *Inside the Prisoner: radical television and film in the 1960s*. BT Batsford, 1998.

Rogers, Dave. *The Prisoner & Danger Man*. Boxtree, 1989.

Sellers, Robert. *Cult TV: The Golden Age of ITC*. Plexus, 2006.

Stevens, Alan & Fiona Moore. *Fall Out: the unofficial and unauthorised guide to The Prisoner*. Telos, 2007.

White, Matthew & Jaffer Ali. *The Official Prisoner Companion*. Warner Books, 1988.

Two prominent websites devoted to the series are:

Six of One – the official appreciation society: www.sixofone.co.uk

The Unmutual: www.theunmutual.co.uk

Thanks to Tim Beddows, Martin Cater, James Chapman, Bruce Clark, Simon Coward, Rick Davy, Dick Fiddy, Larry Hall, Tina Jerke, Roger Langley, Andrew Martin, Anthony McKay, Stephen McKay, Michael Richardson, Julie Rogers and Steve Rogers. Series locations also identified at avengerland.theavengers.tv by Mr and Mrs Beer, Sam Denham, Geoff Dodd, Peter Dunn, Steve Dix, Alan Field, James Hewett, Michael Humphrey, Jeff Morgan, and contributors to the Britmovie Forum and Professional Pilots Rumour Network.

# EPISODE INDEX

The episodes are presented in the order in which they were presented in the original *Synopses and Cast Lists* document issued by ITC in 1967.

Patrick McGoohan *as The Prisoner*
and featuring
Angelo Muscat *as The Butler* [1,3-12,15-17]
with
Peter Swanwick – *The Supervisor* [1,7-11,16-17]

*In the grounds of* The Hotel Portmeirion, Penrhyndeudraeth, North Wales
*by courtesy of* Mr Clough Williams-Ellis [17]
*Script Editor* George Markstein [1-12,16]
*Produced by* David Tomblin
*An ITC Production by Everyman Films Limited*
*Executive Producer* Patrick McGoohan [1-12,14,16]
*Production Manager* Bernard Williams [1-12,16], Ronald Liles [13-15,17]
*Director of Photography* Brendan J Stafford BSC
*Theme by* Ron Grainer
*Musical Director* Albert Elms [2,4,9-15,17]
*Incidental Music* Albert Elms [3,5,8,16]
*Made on Location and at Metro-Goldwyn-Mayer Studios, Borehamwood, England*

## 1   ARRIVAL
*with Guest Stars* Virginia Maskell *as The Woman*, Guy Doleman *as Number Two*, Paul Eddington *as Cobb*, George Baker *as The New Number Two*
*Written by* George Markstein and David Tomblin
*Directed by* Don Chaffey
*ITC Log Line:* Who is he? Who has abducted him? And why? The man who is to remain a prisoner for a long, long time finds himself in a strange world … a world which is menacing and beautiful at the same time.
*First ATV Midlands Broadcast:* Friday 29 September 1967, 7.30pm

## 2   MANY HAPPY RETURNS
*with Guest Stars* Donald Sinden *as The Colonel*, Patrick Cargill *as Thorpe*, Georgina Cookson *as Mrs Butterworth*
*Written by* Anthony Skene
*Directed by* Joseph Serf [Patrick McGoohan]
ITC Log Line: The Prisoner escapes and succeeds in getting back to London. Yet there is still no freedom …
*First ATV Midlands Broadcast:* Friday 10 November 1967, 7.30pm

## 3   A. B. AND C.
*with Guest Stars* Katherine Kath *as Engadine*, Sheila Allen *as Number Fourteen*, Colin Gordon *as Number Two*, Peter Bowles *as 'A'*
*Written by* Anthony Skene
*Directed by* Pat Jackson
*ITC Log Line:* The Prisoner is the subject of an experiment to manipulate his dreams.
*First ATV Midlands Broadcast:* Friday 13 October 1967, 7.30pm

## 4   THE SCHIZOID MAN
*with Guest Stars* Jane Merrow *as Alison*, Anton Rodgers *as Number Two*
*Written by* Terence Feely
*Directed by* Pat Jackson
*ITC Log Line:* Efforts are made to split the Prisoner's personality and make him believe he is someone else.
*First ATV Midlands Broadcast:* Friday 27 October 1967, 7.30pm

## 5   FREE FOR ALL
*with Guest Star* Eric Portman *as Number Two*
*Written by* Paddy Fitz [Patrick McGoohan]
*Directed by* Patrick McGoohan
*ITC Log Line:* The Prisoner stands for election as the new "Number Two", but finds that even a candidate for this top position has no freedom of speech.
*First ATV Midlands Broadcast:* Friday 20 October 1967, 7.30pm

### 6      CHECKMATE

*with Guest Stars* Ronald Radd *as Rook*, Patricia Jessel *as 1st Psychiatrist*, Peter Wyngarde *as Number Two*, Rosalie Crutchley *as Queen*, George Coulouris *as Man with the Stick*
*Written by* Gerald Kelsey
*Directed by* Don Chaffey
*ITC Log Line:* A Queen is the pawn in a grim game of love aimed at breaking the Prisoner.
*First ATV Midlands Broadcast:* Friday 24 November 1967, 7.30pm

### 7      THE CHIMES OF BIG BEN

*with Guest Stars* Leo McKern *as Number Two*, Nadia Gray *as Nadia*, Finlay Currie *as General*, Richard Wattis *as Fotheringay*
*Written by* Vincent Tilsley
*Directed by* Don Chaffey
*ITC Log Line:* The Prisoner learns that it is only a matter of time that foils a dramatic attempt to trap him.
*First ATV Midlands Broadcast:* Friday 6 October 1967, 7.30pm

### 8      THE GENERAL

*with Guest Stars* Colin Gordon *as Number Two*, John Castle *as Number Twelve*, Peter Howell *as Professor*
*Written by* Joshua Adam [Lewis Greifer]
*Directed by* Peter Graham Scott
*ITC Log Line:* Who is the General? Only when he can discover the identity of this mysterious, unseen figure can the Prisoner prove that knowledge is not wisdom.
*First ATV Midlands Broadcast:* Friday 3 November 1967, 7.30pm

### 9      IT'S YOUR FUNERAL

*with Guest Stars* Derren Nesbitt *as New Number Two*, Annette Andre *as Watchmaker's Daughter*, Mark Eden *as Number One Hundred*
*Written by* Michael Cramoy
*Directed by* Robert Asher
*ITC Log Line:* The Prisoner is tricked into "discovering" an assassination plot – but who is going to be killed?
*First ATV Midlands Broadcast:* Friday 8 December 1967, 7.30pm

## 10    HAMMER INTO ANVIL

*with Guest Star* Patrick Cargill *as Number Two*
*Written by* Roger Woddis
*Directed by* Pat Jackson
*ITC Log Line:* The Prisoner, seeking to avenge the death of a persecuted girl, plays a cat-and-mouse game with Number Two, and tricks him into believing that he is a decoy, placed there to spy on him.
*First ATV Midlands Broadcast:* Friday 1 December 1967, 7.30pm

## 11    A CHANGE OF MIND

*with Guest Stars* Angela Browne *as Number Eighty-Six*, John Sharpe *as Number Two*
*Written by* Roger Parkes
*Directed by* Joseph Serf [Patrick McGoohan]
*ITC Log Line:* Can science change a man's mentality? The Prisoner is the subject of a sinister plan to transform his mental processes by sound-waves and drugs, with a beautiful girl as the operator.
*First ATV Midlands Broadcast:* Friday 15 December 1967, 7.30pm

## 12    DANCE OF THE DEAD

*with Guest Stars* Mary Morris *as Number Two*, Duncan MacRae *as Doctor*, Norma West *as Girl Bo-Peep*
*Written by* Anthony Skene
*Directed by* Don Chaffey
*ITC Log Line:* Death lurks amid the gaiety of a carnival, and the Prisoner is put on trial when he makes an audacious bid to foil his captors.
*First ATV Midlands Broadcast:* Friday 17 November 1967, 7.30pm

## 13    THE GIRL WHO WAS DEATH

*with Guest Stars* Kenneth Griffith *as Schnipps*, Justine Lord *as Sonia*
*Written by* Terence Feely. *From an idea by* David Tomblin
*Directed by* David Tomblin
*ITC Log Line:* The Prisoner acts out a fairy-tale with a difference and meets up with a girl who believes they were made for each other: he is a born survivor and she is a born killer. It's quite a challenge!
*First ATV Midlands Broadcast:* Friday 19 January 1968, 7.35pm

### 14    LIVING IN HARMONY

*with Guest Stars* Alexis Kanner *as The Kid*, David Bauer *as The Judge*, Valerie French *as Kathy*

*From a Story by* David Tomblin and Ian L Rakoff.

*Written and Directed by* David Tomblin.

*ITC Log Line:* The Prisoner finds himself in a Western township, tricked into becoming sheriff – but can he be forced into carrying a gun and into killing?

*First ATV Midlands Broadcast:* Friday 29 December 1967, 7.30pm

### 15    DO NOT FORSAKE ME OH MY DARLING

*with Guest Stars* Zena Walker *as Janet*, Clifford Evans *as Number Two*, Nigel Stock *as The Colonel*

*Written by* Vincent Tilsley

*Directed by* Pat Jackson

*ITC Log Line:* The Prisoner undergoes an eerie transformation which transmits his mind and personality into another man's body.

*First ATV Midlands Broadcast:* Friday 22 December 1967, 7.30pm

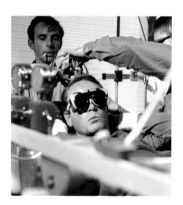

### 16    ONCE UPON A TIME

*with Guest Star* Leo McKern *as Number Two*

*Written and Directed by* Patrick McGoohan

*ITC Log Line:* The Prisoner faces ruthless interrogation, taken to the extreme degree, in an effort to make him reveal why he resigned from his top secret job. One man must break …

*First ATV Midlands Broadcast:* Friday 26 January 1968, 7.35pm

### 17    FALL OUT

*with Guest Stars* Leo McKern, Kenneth Griffith *as The President*, Alexis Kanner

*Written and Directed by* Patrick McGoohan

*ITC Log Line:* The Prisoner comes to the end of his nightmarish adventure.

*First Broadcast:* Thursday 1 February 1968, 7.30pm [Scottish];

*First ATV Midlands Broadcast:* Friday 2 February 1968, 7.30pm